LANGUAGE AND LEARNING IN THE DIGITAL AGE

In *Language and Learning in the Digital Age*, linguist James Paul Gee and educator Elisabeth Hayes deal with the forces unleashed by today's digital media, forces that are transforming language and learning for good and ill.

They argue that the role of oral language is almost always entirely misunderstood in debates about digital media. Like the earlier inventions of writing and print, digital media actually "power up" or enhance the powers of oral language.

Gee and Hayes deal, as well, with current digital transformations of language and literacy in the context of a growing crisis in traditional schooling in developed countries. With the advent of new forms of digital media, children are increasingly drawn towards video games, social media, and alternative ways of learning. Gee and Hayes explore the way in which these alternative methods of learning can be a force for a paradigm change in schooling.

This is an engaging, accessible read both for undergraduate and graduate students and for scholars in language, linguistics, education, media and communication studies.

James Paul Gee is the Mary Lou Fulton Presidential Professor of Literacy Studies at Arizona State University, USA. He is a member of the National Academy of Education, and author of numerous books, including the bestselling *An Introduction to Discourse Analysis* (Routledge, 3rd edn, 2011) and companion title *How to do Discourse Analysis* (Routledge, 2011).

Elisabeth R. Hayes is Professor of English at Arizona State University, USA.

"*Language and Learning in the Digital Age* is both grounded and wise. Gee and Hayes' perspective is one that looks back as much as it looks forward and it has a place on everyone's bookshelf or digital reader, so that we can take stock in how far we have come (and how far we have to go)."

Jennifer Rowsell, *Canada Research Chair in Multiliteracies, Brock University, Canada*

"Both a stimulating and highly readable account of how new media are changing the way we communicate and learn and an antidote to the various moral panics surrounding computers, the Internet and youth culture. This book should be required reading for anyone working in education today."

Rodney Jones, *City University of Hong Kong*

LANGUAGE AND LEARNING IN THE DIGITAL AGE

James Paul Gee and Elisabeth R. Hayes

Routledge
Taylor & Francis Group

LONDON AND NEW YORK

First published 2011
by Routledge
2 Park Square, Milton Park, Abingdon, Oxon OX14 4RN

Simultaneously published in the USA and Canada
by Routledge
711 Third Avenue, New York, NY 10017

Routledge is an imprint of the Taylor & Francis Group, an informa business

Typeset in Bembo and ITC Stone Sans by
Bookcraft Ltd, Stroud, Gloucestershire
Printed and bound in the United States of America
by Edwards Brothers, Inc.

British Library Cataloguing in Publication Data
A catalogue record for this book is available from the British Library

Library of Congress Cataloging in Publication Data
Gee, James Paul.
Language and learning in the digital age / James Paul Gee and Elisabeth Hayes.
— 1st ed.
  p. cm.
Includes bibliographical references.
1. Language and languages—Study and teaching. 2. Digital media.
3. Social media. I. Hayes, Elisabeth. II. Title.
P51.G344 2010
418.0078'5—dc22   2010034570

ISBN 13: 978-0-415-60276-1 (hbk)
ISBN 13: 978-0-415-60277-8 (pbk)
ISBN 13: 978-0-203-83091-8 (ebk)

For Natasha 2007–2010

"Only connect ..."

Epigraph to E. M. Forster's 1910 novel *Howards End*

CONTENTS

1
INTRODUCTION

In a title like *Language and Learning in the Digital Age*, the word "language" seems less trendy than the word "digital." We are rightly impressed by our new digital tools. Their perils and possibilities are new. In comparison, language seems so old and mundane, its perils and possibilities long forgotten. However, we will argue that the perils and possibilities of digital media are, in fact, species of the same perils and possibilities we find in the history of oral language and written language.

Digital media are an interesting hybrid of the properties of oral language and of written language. Oral language is interactive but ephemeral (sound passes away quickly). It does not travel accurately because each person in a chain of communication can easily change it. Literacy is less interactive but permanent. It travels far and wide and it is harder to change as pieces of paper or books are passed down through a chain of people.

When digital media carry language, language can be interactive, for example in a chat room, via text messaging, or on a Twitter feed, but also permanent. It can travel far and wide, but can be changed even more rapidly and thoroughly than a rumor as each user has a chance to modify it, for example, in wikis. We will argue that digital media "power up" or enhance the powers of language, oral and written, just as written language "powered up" or enhanced the powers of oral language.

Readers may say that digital media carry so much more than language. But language itself is and has always been a mixture of sound, words, images created in the mind, and gestures used in contexts full of objects, sounds, actions, and interactions. Language has always been "multimodal" (combining words, images, and sounds) as are many messages conveyed via digital media and, indeed, many other media today.

Nevertheless, multimodality is more pervasive, diverse, and important today than ever before. A comparison between a textbook or a newspaper from the 1950s and today will show that today's textbooks and newspapers have many more images in them (Lemke 1998). Both textbooks and newspapers are often available today on the Internet where they are accompanied by yet more images and video.

Multitasking is another pervasive and important phenomenon today. Multitasking by the so-called "digital generation" is much discussed. However, oral language has always demanded multitasking. In speaking we have to pay attention, as we will see, to a myriad of things. The same is true of early hunting and gathering by our ancestors. The last humans who could not multitask died out long ago, for good Darwinian reasons. Nonetheless, today multitasking is required more than ever and the ability to know how, when, and where to multitask is becoming paramount.

Digital media are a delivery system for language (and other things), just like a car is a delivery system for humans. Written language was an earlier delivery system for language. We can hardly understand a delivery system if we do not understand what it carries and why. While we may seem to trivialize digital media and written language by calling them delivery systems, in reality we do no such thing. Cars, trucks, planes, and tanks are delivery systems for humans, but they have transformed the world and human beings for both good and bad.

This book is about *language* in the digital age. So let's talk about language. Oral language was a gift to humans from evolution, culture, or God (depending on your point of view). It was a gift of true equality. Everyone, barring very severe disorders or terrible social circumstances, acquires a native language (Chomsky 1986; Pinker 1994). Furthermore, every human is both a producer (a talker) and a consumer (a listener) when it comes to oral language (or sign language, for that matter).

Cultures, in all likelihood not long after they first arose, had a problem with this equality. In many cultures, it came to pass that the powerful restricted other people's rights to speak. The powerful set themselves up as the official spokespersons for the culture. Kings, elders, and shamans came to produce the official and powerful speech in cultures. Everyday people became, when speech was truly consequential, consumers (listeners) and not producers (speakers). They were, in matters of consequence, often silenced.

By the Middle Ages in the West, society was thoroughly organized into a "great chain of being" (Lovejoy 1933) with kings and bishops at the top, knights and lords below them, followed by land owners and tradespeople, and, at the bottom, the majority of the population, peasants. This was a chain as much about who had the authority to speak and to speak the truth and who did not, than it was of internal worth. It was about who should listen to whom. Peasants, at the bottom, listened to everyone else and spoke authoritatively to none.

Writing created a new challenge to authority and struck a new blow for equality. When someone speaks out, authority can easily identify and reach that person to enforce power. But when someone writes on a wall, a building, or a piece of paper, they can be anonymous and they can be miles away by the time the authorities read what they wrote.

Writing once again offered the possibility that all could be both producers (writers) and consumers (readers). It offered people the capacity to confront authority from anonymity and from afar. When print came along, the possibilities just became infinitely larger, since now books could be more easily produced, made more cheaply, and distributed to many more people. But literacy was fated never really to work this way, save for in special circumstances.

In the case of both handwritten manuscripts and printed books, reading was, until modern times, restricted to the well-off, the educated, and the powerful in most countries (Graff 1979, 1987). When countries like Sweden achieved nearly universal reading (in the sixteenth century), reading was encouraged so that all could read the Bible and ministers visited homes to ensure that everyone was reading "correctly" (Johansson 1977). In modern societies, even when reading became nearly universal, writing spread much more slowly and never became universal. Many people today cannot write nearly as well as they can read. Printing houses and publishers, almost from the beginning of print, controlled what could be officially published (often along with state authorities). Once again, everyday people were meant to consume (read) and not produce (write, and certainly not publish).

Digital media again offer us an opportunity for equality, for letting everyone be producers as well as consumers. With digital media people can often bypass official institutions and oversight to produce their own media, knowledge, products, services, and texts. They can easily distribute their productions worldwide. They can make ads, movies, and video games to compete with the "professionals" or to critique "mainstream" sources. Through the Internet, even people once considered "marginal" or not "mainstream" can find many others like themselves across the globe and group together. People without official credentials can debate those who do have them and compete with them to produce knowledge and ideas.

Since we know that, with both oral language and literacy, the ability of the powerless to produce and not just consume was curtailed, restricted, and policed, though never with total success, we can suspect that forces will arise to stem the tide of everyday production and participation that digital media have unleashed. Digital media are still new enough that the shape these controls will take is not fully clear, even to the powerful, nor can we be sure that this time equality will not win out.

Equality is a big problem for all of us, not just those who want to hold power over others. If everyone has a point of view and the ability to voice (or write) it, in a big enough group, there is not time or attention enough for everyone to be heard. Not everyone can get a significant audience and those who do will gain more status and power. So far, quality and truth have certainly not determined by themselves who gets a big audience, status, or power.

The same problem arises in an even more dramatic form with digital media, since today audiences can be global. In an age where everyone can produce and appeal to the whole world for an audience, some people gain a big audience and some do not, since none of us can pay attention to even a small fraction of the production, information, and communication circulating today in our global, interconnected media.

It is true, though, that thanks to how big the potential audience is these days (namely everyone with a computational device, mobile or not, and a connection to the Internet), even small causes, crackpots, and people with rare skills and insights can find a significant audience, though not a mass one. Everyone who loves making doll heads out of avocado pits can find each other around the world and group together as "people like us" or "people with a shared passion" (that others do not understand). Before they felt alone among those who thought they were odd, special, or marginal.

This ability to gain an audience at all, even if not a mass one, is in many respects good and to be encouraged and applauded. Today, people with rare diseases or formerly lost causes can find and get support from others. Young people can gain readers for their fan fiction from across the world. Their readership won't compare with popular published authors, but they often don't care, since they are writing for the love of it and adore having readers at all.

But there is a potential downside as well. As the ability for people to find others with the same interests or passions increases, so do the number of groups. People can splinter and even polarize around their favored passions, values, and even political views, communicating only with others who share their passions, values, and views. The irony becomes that in a world where everyone can produce and find an audience, "everyone" becomes not a true public or civil space, but a bunch of groups "doing their own thing." Equality is further jeopardized in this world when some people have better access than others to the groups whose interests or passions lead to more status and success in society.

Today, despite the proliferating groups on the Internet and the heavily polarized politics in the United States and some other countries (caused in part by the growth in media and group sites that allow everyone to customize what they hear only to what they already believe), there are many instances where people from different groups have used the Internet and social media to engage in large-scale public causes, whether fighting dictators or aiding people in disasters. It remains to be seen how the tension will play out between the trend to split into many different, valued-laden groups and the opportunity for people to organize for large causes more spontaneously than ever before.

We have hope and fear. Hope that diversity and commonality, as well as production and consumption, can finally find a happy marriage. Fear that control over everyday producers will be re-asserted, groups will splinter and polarize, and common cause and a public sphere (both nationally and globally) will erode or become dominated only by the technologically elite.

There is one crucial point we want to make before readers begin this book in earnest. It is popular today for people to write books to say that some aspect of digital media (social media, the Internet, video games, and so forth) is bad or ruining our culture or endangering our civilization (e.g. among many others, Bauerline 2008 or Carr 2010). There are others who think that digital media are a panacea; for example, they think that just by giving poor children computers and the Internet we could close the gap in school performance between the rich and the poor (but see Stross 2010).

No technology—books, television, computers, video games, or the Internet—by itself makes people good or bad, smart or stupid. Such technologies have effects only in terms of how, when, where, and why they are put to use. They have different effects in different contexts of use. They can be forces for good or ill. A computer connected to the Internet in the hands of a child with good mentoring is often a force for learning. It may not be in other circumstances. The real issue, then, is social, that is, who has and who does not have mentoring, not technology alone. The same is true of books and of language, as we will see.

The New Testament (John 1:1) says: "In the beginning was the Word, and the Word was with God, and the Word was God." For humans, that first word was spoken. Oral language is our original gift. Written language came along much later. Digital media later still. For centuries people identified the breath with which we speak with the spirit or the soul and the language they spoke with their unique humanity. Written language froze that breath, allowing it to travel far and wide, allowing the growth of cities, empires, and institutions. Digital media have unfrozen it again, creating a voice that can travel far and rapidly among "everyday people" and, for good and ill, challenge the power of experts, empires, and institutions. What will happen? Only the future will tell.

2

LANGUAGE

What is language?

The word "language" can mean different things. One way we can think about language is as something in our heads. We can think of it as a set of "rules" in our minds or brains that tells us how to speak "grammatically." In this sense, language is a cognitive phenomenon (Clark 1996).

We can also view language as something physically present in the world. It is present in the form of speech, audio recordings, and writings. In this sense, language is a material object.

Alternatively, we can view language as a set of social conventions, shared by a group of people, about how to communicate (Duranti 1997). This is rather like baseball: baseball is based on a set of rules and, while these rules are in people's heads and in rule books, what is most important about them is that they are followed by people when they play the game.

Of course, the conventions for spoken language are not really in a rule book of any kind. Some books about grammar tell us how their authors think people should (but don't always) talk, while other books seek to describe how people actually do talk. Children don't read books of either sort to learn how to talk.

The conventions that children learn to follow in speaking are social (Halliday & Hasan 1989). They are social in the sense that we catch on to them, in large part, by imitating other people (though with some variation).

Language can be viewed as cognitive, material, or social; it is, of course, all of these at one and the same time. Language is also something that is both individual and social. Language seems to belong to us as individuals—to be something we can use in distinctive ways—and yet seems also to be shaped by social conventions beyond our individual control. As an individual, I can say what no one else has ever said before. My language, my way of communicating, seems to be my own. I can say, for instance: "Blue cows decry metaphysics on Tuesdays" and probably this has never been said (or written) before by anyone else.

At the same time, my language (English) was here long before I arrived on the scene. Many others have used it before me, and I follow much the same conventions others have followed. I use many words and phrases that I have heard or read before. Thus, when I said "Blue cows decry metaphysics on Tuesdays" I followed a grammatical pattern that other English speakers have long followed (Subject Verb Object). Furthermore, I was influenced by a sentence the linguist Noam Chomsky (1957: 15) once wrote (making much the same point I was trying to make with my "novel" sentence: people can say totally novel things): "Green ideas sleep furiously." When I wrote the sentence, I thought "decry metaphysics" was pretty novel, but I later found that the phrase has 151 hits on Google.

Other people's language is inside my head whether I know it or not. Looked at this way, language is a communal resource from which we all beg, borrow, and steal. People talk like others and still each of us has our own unique style (Bakhtin 1981, 1986).

Oral and written language

We often distinguish among "oral language," "written language," and "language" (as a term that includes both oral and written language). We can even use the term language for "languages" that are not human, as in "the language of the bees" or, if human, languages that are not "natural," as in "the language of mathematics."

For humans, language was oral long before it was written. Oral language has existed since the dawn of humanity. Written language was invented much more recently; estimates range from 3000 to 8000 years ago (Sampson 1990), and it was invented only by a few different cultures (Goody 1986, 1988).

All human groups have oral language. Not all cultures have had or even today have written language. Oral language was language's first and primary form. Distinguishing between oral and written language, and thinking about oral language as in some sense primary, is necessary to identify the distinctive features of each.

Who or what made language?

We know that people invented the conventions of baseball consciously (which is why we call them "rules"). They also agree to change them consciously and after overt discussion. Given these rules, some people are good at baseball and some are not.

Language is not like baseball in either of these respects. No group of humans got together and consciously decided what the conventions (or rules) of language would be. Furthermore, all humans are good at learning their first language and can learn any language in the world equally easily as their first language (Chomsky 1986; Pinker 1994).

All human languages share basic design properties (Chomsky 1957, 1986; Comrie 1981; Greenberg 1978). They all have vowels and consonants and syllables.

They all have nouns, verbs, sentences, and clauses grammatically. They all have "recursion" (the potential to make longer and longer sentences by embedding one phrase or clause in another, as in: "John thinks that Mary believes that Sue claimed that Bob warned Jane not to believe that chimps are our ancestors"—obviously this could go on forever). Languages can all form questions, make statements, and give orders, and the ways they do these things are similar in some respects. There are yet deeper language universals that are beyond our scope here.

It is highly likely that all human languages developed from one original language. Over a long period of time, as different human groups spread across the world and communicated only with each other, this original language changed in different ways in different places. This gave rise to the great diversity in human languages that we see today and that was once even richer (before so many languages died out).

Language evolved as a capacity in human beings along with the growth of human cultures. We do not know what early stages of human language were like, since there are no early or "primitive" languages left. All human languages are complex and the languages spoken by cultures with no literacy are not less complex syntactically than those spoken by cultures with literacy (Gee 2004; Pinker 1994).

Barring severe disabilities or social problems, all humans acquire language as a core or basic property of their humanity. The form of language they acquire we can call their "vernacular" (Gee 2004). A vernacular variety of language is the form of language people use in their "everyday" lives when they are not speaking as specialists or experts of any sort. Even experts speak a vernacular variety of their language when they are not speaking or acting as experts.

People's vernacular style of language varies by dialect (so the vernacular form of English is different in different parts of the country or among different social groups). However, everyone's vernacular variety is equally complex and equally English (or whatever other language they have acquired).

In the course of history, people have invented new styles of speaking or writing for specific special purposes. They had a specific job to do and designed changes to the language to get it done. These varieties of a language use the grammatical resources of vernacular varieties, but are specialist varieties that not everyone learns or knows (while everyone has a vernacular variety).

So, for example, imagine a culture wants to engage in religious rituals of some sort. They have (culturally) designed certain ceremonies, environments, and artifacts for their rituals. They may also design changes to their language so they can use that language for their rituals, just as they use their ceremonies, environments, and artifacts. They create a "religious language" or a "ritual language," ways of using language for ritual or religious purposes.

Later in history, people (as groups, cultures, societies, institutions, and even clubs) have created a massive number of varieties of language. They have changed their basic language to engage in language varieties for mathematics, science, law, medicine, engineering, game design, anime fandom, and many other things.

To sum up: language developed as a capacity in humans (and not other animals) in the course of human evolution and then it was transformed by cultures as they invented new varieties of language for special purposes. Children acquire a vernacular variety of their first language as part of the process of being socialized into their families and communities. They are equally good at this, since the process is partly controlled by their biological capacity for acquiring language, a capacity special to humans. All children later have to learn specialized varieties of language, like the language of physics or of carpenters, more overtly and with more variation among learners.

Oral language

In this book we will eventually argue that digital media are a powerful force, not to lessen the importance of language, but to "level up," or enhance, language. Digital media "power up" (improve and expand) abilities language already has and they give language new abilities, or new powers. In that way, they are doing to language what human cultures have always done since they inherited language.

But it is important now to stop and talk, again, about what we mean by "language." Language arose first as speech (oral language). Oral language is language's original and primary form. It is oral language that evolved in the human species.

Oral language arose a long time ago, long enough for evolution to transform it. Writing did not. Writing is a relatively recent invention (Goody 1986, 1988). It has not been around long enough to be a product of evolution. It was purely a cultural invention (as is the language of mathematics or of *Yu-Gi-Oh!*). It was an invention of only very few cultures and then spread to others. All cultures initially and most cultures historically were "oral cultures" in the sense that they had no writing. There are still some oral cultures today.

For most of human history, oral language was used for face-to-face communication where people were co-present with each other in space and time. But think about what happened when humans invented the technology of audio recording. Now the oral word could be used for communication across time and space when people were not face-to-face or co-present. They could even listen to the recorded voice of a dead person.

Phones, too, allowed people to talk and respond at a distance (though not if they were dead). Today, voice chat through computers (in a game like *World of WarCraft* or in something like Skype) allows people to talk to others across the globe in real time in small or large groups without being physically co-present. If we add video to voice chat, we get a new form of co-presence at a distance. It's all oral language, but greatly enhanced and empowered in comparison to "face-to-face co-present-in-local-space-and-time communication."

Such technological changes in oral language, while they are enhancements and empowerments in some senses, do involve losses. We will see that all technological changes involve both gains and losses. A person can speak on a tape, but we cannot speak to that person. They cannot be challenged and they cannot talk back. A dialogic property of face-to-face communication has been lost. Phones lose visual cues and even video-enhanced voice chat loses some of the timing and close embodiment that is important to face-to-face communication.

Of course, we have not given up face-to-face co-present local communication and we still reap its benefits. Nonetheless, new forms of technologically enhanced communication do change the "ecology" of such face-to-face co-present local communication. For example, many people spend more time talking to people from across the world via voice chat, Skype, and chat rooms than they do talking to their neighbors in face-to-face co-present local communication.

In the next chapter we will discuss the nature of oral language in more depth. There we will argue that "oral" is not really an appropriate word here. There are also human languages (which bear all the hallmarks of language's original design properties) that are signed, not spoken. We can all think with language in our minds and not say it (though thinking language is somewhat like mentally saying it or signing it to oneself).

The spatial basis of meaning in language and thinking

As language evolved in human beings, what were its core or essential properties? The origins of language are so long in the past that we know next to nothing about them. Early humans were hunters and gatherers. Surely, when language first arose, humans used it for face-to-face communication and to talk about the here and now and things physically present around them ("Look, antelope, over there" accompanied by a gesture). This here-and-now aspect of language is, and always has been, at the very foundation of human language.

Early humans surely did not sit around the fire talking about metaphysics or the emotional nuances (or lack thereof) of the male brain. Life in those early days, to adopt a well-known phrase from Thomas Hobbes, was "nasty, brutish, and short." Our ancestors were focused on survival. Early language almost certainly was used only to communicate about concrete matters in the here and now, not abstract matters.

Thus, an initial function of language was to allow human beings to talk about concrete things in the here and now while being face-to-face with others. Gesture was probably an important accompaniment of language at this point (as it still is today). Let's call this the Spatial Property of Language. A core property of language is its use for face-to-face communication about concrete things in the here and now.

As language evolved further and eventually was transformed by human culture, this original Spatial Property became more powerful in an interesting way. Humans learned to talk about abstract and mental things and they did so by talking about them as if they were things in space and time. People, through language, began to treat things which are not actually concrete and in the here and now as if they were, through metaphor (Anderson 1971; Lakoff 1987; Lakoff & Johnson 1980; Lyons 1977). People also think about abstract things as if they were concrete, since people often use language to think (Lakoff 1987). People, in talk and thought, move from the concrete to the abstract.

For example, when I say, "I lost my keys," I am talking about a physical thing in space. When I say, "I lost my mind," "I lost my integrity," "I lost my train of thought," or "I lost the election," I am talking about things that are more abstract than my keys and not physical (or at least a simple physical thing) like my keys. These are all metaphors. We treat minds, integrity, thought, and elections as if they are things I can misplace in space (Lakoff 1987; Lakoff & Johnson 1980). There are many examples of such spatial metaphors:

PHYSICAL	**ABSTRACT OR MENTAL**
I dropped my keys.	The idea just dropped out of my head.
Drop that gun!	Drop that topic!
I went away from home.	I went insane.
I came back home.	I came back to my senses.
I explored the park.	I explored algebra.
I moved the book.	The speech moved me emotionally.
I found a dollar bill.	I found the truth.
I slipped on the ice.	The idea slipped my mind.
John grew six inches.	John grew as a statesman.
I gained in stature (height).	I gained in stature (reputation).
The cab drove me home.	He drives me crazy.
Nothing is in the box.	Nothing is in his head.
I pushed the cart.	I pushed the idea.
Birds fly.	That proposal is not going to fly.

Over time, the Spatial Property (the ability to talk about concrete things in the here and now) was also the basis for talking about mental and abstract things via metaphors. Once humans hit on this metaphorical trick of talking about mental and abstract things as if they were things in space and time, they were on the path to being able to talk about metaphysics, minds, and the emotional nuances (or lack thereof) of males' brains. The move from talk about concrete things in the here and to talk about mental and abstract things was a major step in the development of the human mind, human culture, and human language.

In this book we will discuss many other important changes in language. We will watch language become more powerful, just as it did when spatial metaphors were used to talk about abstract and mental things. We will see that digital media are causing important changes in language. But the most powerful enhancement of language in human history was literacy—written language. Literacy is a technology, just like digital media. So far, its effects dwarf those of digital media; one of the key ways digital media have and will transform language is by transforming or replacing literacy in various spheres and practices. We will turn to literacy in the next chapter.

Being embodied and situated

Though a popular belief was that humans think through abstractions and gener-alities, in reality, humans think through images and experiences (Clark 1989; Gee 2004). Consider the difference between "The coffee spilled, go get a mop" and "The coffee spilled, go get a broom" (Clark 1989). You readily recall a world of experience, not just definitions of words, to understand these sentences.

When we need to understand abstractions, or things that are too small, too large, or too complex for us to perceive or understand easily, we often call on the power of metaphors to describe them. We see, for example, a biological cell as a little room full of little machines making things. We picture the inside of an atom as if it were composed of little planets orbiting around a central body (the nucleus). We imagine DNA as if it was a blueprint for a house. Our metaphors can get us into trouble, but they are, nonetheless, often essential for human understanding. Scientists' models are often like metaphors: for example, the wire frame model of the double helix of DNA, a model plane in a wind tunnel, a diagram of the forces impinging on a moving object, the picture of a branching tree to represent evolution.

Understanding in thought and language is, for us humans, first and foremost embodied and situated. We see and understand things through the perspective of our bodies (embodied) and in terms of specific contexts and variations across contexts (situated). For humans, understanding very small things (like atoms) and very big ones (like galaxies) is hard since they are beyond our ordinary means of perception. Understanding things that are more accessible to our senses is much easier for us. We have had to invent quite special tools to understand the very small and the very large.

We have, though only in a sense and with real limitations, freed ourselves from our bodies, from concreteness, and from the here and now. We have tools to deal with abstraction that are no longer tied to metaphor (e.g. various branches of math-ematics). The technology that freed us the most from the here and now was literacy. Literacy allowed language to be uncoupled from conversation among humans in specific contexts of use. It allowed for the invention of specialized languages to deal with abstract and complex things.

Digital media (like text messaging, Twitter, and other social media) are, in a sense, bringing language back to its conversational, interactive, here-and-now foundations. They are also bringing back concrete images and experiences, as well as metaphors, for understanding the abstract and the complex through, for example, simulations and video games. But they are doing this in quite different ways than did oral language.

People with today's social media and virtual worlds can "chat" (in writing or in voice chat) with people across the world. Such interactions are embodied, situated, and "face-to-face" in a new way.

Digital media also create new ways to use models and metaphors for under-standing. They allow us, in a simulation or a game, to become an electron and move through an electromagnetic field, to be a virus entering a body, the leader of a wolf

Language **13**

pack, or a firefly signaling to a mate. The scale of our human bodies is no longer the limitation it once was. We can use simulations and games as models or metaphors for understanding (Gee 2007b, 2007c).

With literacy, language is separated from bodies. With digital media the body often returns, but in displaced and virtual ways. We understand an electromagnetic field through a concrete embodied experience, but our (surrogate) "body" is an electron. We understand modern warfare on the field of battle, but the field is virtual and the body is an avatar we control through virtual space and time.

Language returns to a landscape of voice, the here and now, to concrete embodied understandings, to images and metaphors, and to "face-to-face" individualized interactions. But this is a landscape unlike what has come before.

3

LITERACY

What is language? What is literacy?

The word "literacy" is used in many different ways. We will use it in a narrow and traditional sense. By "literacy" we will mean reading and writing human language.

More extended uses of the term (e.g. "computer literacy," "emotional literacy," "science literacy") are fine for other purposes. However, in this book, we keep the notion of literacy narrow and traditional so that we can first understand the role of literacy and then the role of digital media in changing language. Understanding how literacy as a technology has influenced language is important for understanding later how digital media as technologies influence language.

Before we can discuss literacy coherently, we need (perhaps surprisingly) to be clear about what we mean by "oral language." Ironically, oral language isn't always oral (audible, spoken). As we mentioned in the previous chapter, we can talk to ourselves silently and we often use language to think (which may itself be a form of silent speaking).

American Sign Language (ASL) is signed, not spoken, but it is a real language just like English or Spanish (Gee & Goodhart 1988; Grosjean & Lane 1980). By the way, we are not talking about "Signed English," but about ASL acquired as a native language by deaf children.

Whether language is spoken to others out loud or silently to oneself, it is inherently interactive or dialogic. If I say or think to myself, "Is there really any reason for me to have shown up today?," the very form of my silent utterance is a question that invites a response, namely an answer to the question—which, of course, I might or might not actually give to myself. If I say or think to myself, "That guy really is a fool," my silent utterance is a claim that invites a response to questions like "How do you know that?" "Are you being too hard on him?" and so forth. Again, I may skip the response or engage in an internal dialogue, but language is built to be interactive and to invite certain sorts of responses or dialogue.

Speaking is just one way to express language. Thinking is another way and signing is yet another way. Speech, thinking, and signing are different *delivery systems* for language. They are *not* themselves language. Literacy is yet another delivery system for language. It, too, is not itself language. So what is "language," this thing that can be delivered orally, through thinking, by signing, or in writing?

Language is a set of social conventions about how to combine words, phrases, clauses, and sentences to communicate meanings. These grammatical combinations of words ("grammatical sentences") are delivered or expressed via speech, thought, signing, or writing. Language is a "system" of conventions about how to make meanings that can be expressed or delivered in different ways.

For human beings, the original and primary form of language is language spoken (or signed) to others (Gee 2004, 2008a; Pinker 1994). Writing is a latecomer on the scene and exists to deliver language that is or can be oral, thought, or signed (Botha & Knight 2009; Gee 2004; Goody 1986, 1988; Olson 1996; Snow 1991).

Not all spoken language can be expressed through writing systems. For example, the rise and fall in the pitch of the voice that characterize intonation contours in English have no systematic symbols in the English writing system. Nor do the changes in stress that distinguish a word like "record" (I kept a record of our conversation) and "record" (I will not record our conversation). No writing system can capture all of the features of speech (or thought or signing) that are relevant to communication and meaning.

Writing is a secondary delivery system, delivering language that can be spoken, thought, or signed. For the rest of this book, we will use the term "oral language" to mean language that is delivered by speech, thinking, or signing, and the term "written language" to be language that is delivered by writing. To say writing is secondary does not mean literacy is not important, but it does mean that oral language is more foundational for literacy and literacy learning than many people realize (Gee 2004; Hart & Risely 1995; Heath 1983; Scollon & Scollon 1981).

Stating that literacy is a delivery system for oral language, and a secondary one at that, may seem to downplay its significance. But, in reality, it does not. Consider automobiles, which are a "delivery system" for human beings. Cars are not themselves human beings, but they have radically changed how humans act, interact, think, plan, and value. The impact they have had on our cities and on the world economically, culturally, and environmentally is massive. Far from being trivial, since they are "only" a delivery system, automobiles are transformative. Literacy, too, has been transformative of both language and human beings.

There is yet another way to view the impact of literacy as a delivery system for language. When humans have a tool, like a gun, a pole vault pole in pole vaulting, or a forklift in an industrial plant, the human being is capable of doing more with the tool than without it (Wertsch 1998). Human ability is so enhanced with tools that we can see the "person-with-tool" as an integrated entity; that is, we can see the actor in pole vaulting as "human-with-pole" (pole-vaulter), the actor using a forklift as "human-with-forklift" (forklift operator), and the actor with a gun as "human-with-gun" (gunman).

So, too, when we think about literacy, we could see the "actor" as "human-with-writing" or, even, in a sense, as "human-with-language-with-literacy." Human beings and language are both capable of different things with literacy than without it (Havelock 1976, 1986; Olson 1996; Ong 1982; Street 1984).

Literacy

In many countries, reading is seen as an essential skill for an educated person. In the United States we have had, over the years, a number of "reading wars," and some other countries have had them as well (Coles 2000; National Reading Panel 2000). These wars have been conflicts over how to teach reading to young children in school.

One side of the war (see Gee 2008b for a discussion of both sides) says that oral language and literacy are both "language." Since children learn oral language through immersion in communication and socialization early on in life (they do not need any overt teaching), it is argued that children should learn literacy the same way. They should be immersed in meaningful practices where they use literacy for authentic communication.

The other side argues that oral language and literacy are different things. Oral language arose long ago in the course of human evolution, while literacy arose relatively recently as a cultural invention. This side argues that, unlike oral language, literacy needs to be overtly taught as a skill that is not "natural" to children in the way oral language is.

Both sides of the reading wars are wrong and right. Literacy is not "language" in the sense that oral language is. It is a delivery system for oral language (or thought language or sign language, remember). There is a role for overt teaching in literacy (and none in the acquisition of one's native language, though this does not stop some parents from trying).

However, literacy (using writing as a delivery system for language) is, indeed, acquired through socialization (in the family and in school) and through authentic practice and not just, or even mainly, overt instruction (Gee 2004; Heath 1983). Children become members of a "literate culture" (actually one version or another depending on their communities) through enculturation (Gee 2004; Heath 1983; Scollon & Scollon 1981; Street 1984). This is how children learn other cultural skills, like cooking, storytelling, and video gaming. Instruction plays a role, but takes a back seat to being socialized with others as a member of a culturally or at least socially distinctive group of people.

Children from homes that do not enculturate them early into some version of literate culture (and a version that ensures they do well at school, given how schools actually function) come to school in need of more practice and immersion in literacy activities than the school usually has the time or will to provide. Unfortunately, such children typically are given large doses of overt instruction and often skill-and-drill. This approach is not optimal for helping children form a deep affiliation with literacy as an "identity" (being a literate person, lifelong reader, committed writer, and so forth), though it often succeeds in preparing children to pass tests.

Certain parts of the human brain are used for both (oral) language and literacy. For example, many parts of the brain devoted to comprehension are involved with the use of language as well as literacy. These parts of the brain are used, as well, to comprehend things and activities in the world. Comprehension is a multi-purpose process not tied to language or literacy alone (Barsalou 1999; Kintsch 1998).

What makes oral language distinctive is that it has been shaped for face-to-face communication and thought, for example, for internal dialogues with ourselves (Tomasello 1999). This is also its deepest limitation. Oral language fades as soon as it is spoken or thought. It leaves no record. Even if we think we remember what we have previously thought or said to ourselves, we cannot be sure our memory is correct since there is no independent way to check it. We will see below how technologies are called on to make up for this limitation.

What makes literacy distinctive is that, as a code or delivery system for oral language, it can transmit meanings far beyond face-to-face contacts. It also can serve as a record that can be checked by multiple people. But this is literacy's deepest limitation as well: it can be used in ways the author never intended or wished.

The phrase "written language" can be misleading. It actually means "a written version of oral language." Written language is, in some sense, "frozen" oral language, though it has capabilities that oral language does not. English, like many other languages, is written with an alphabet, one of the most ingenious and important inventions of human culture (Havelock 1976; Olson 1996; Pattison 1982). An alphabet uses letters to represent the sounds of words. English has about 44 "phonemes" (individual speech sounds that distinguish words from each other). The English alphabet uses only 26 letters to represent these 44 sounds. The 26 letters represent thousands and thousands of words, a near miracle of efficiency.

An alphabet is a code for preserving oral language. It is a code by which literate speakers can decipher how to "say" (to others or to themselves) what is being written, though, of course, they do not have to say it, at least not out loud. Such codes can vary quite a bit. For example, there are writing systems that do not use alphabets, but instead use written symbols for syllables, not individual sounds. Thus, a two-syllable word like "wonder" would be represented by two symbols instead of six symbols (letters). Such systems require more symbols than an alphabet, but otherwise they represent words by representing how they are said, just like in alphabetic writing, since syllables are a unit of sound, not meaning.

There are also writing systems that represent meanings (really the morphemes of a language) directly and not sounds or syllables. For example, a round symbol could stand for a circle or the sun (or, if the system is not iconic, an arbitrary symbol could be used for "sun" and another for "son"). Such writing systems are not codes for oral language. They do not tell speakers how to say what is written. However, such systems are not very efficient either, since they need thousands of symbols for thousands of different meanings, while an alphabet needs only a couple of dozen symbols or so.

Such writing systems usually change over time to incorporate symbols that signal, at least some of the time, the word in the oral language the meaning is associated with. Even these meaning-driven, rather than sound-driven, writing systems encode meanings that speakers of the language can say in words. In fact, speakers of different languages can say them in their different languages, since the symbols stand for meanings and not the sounds of words in any one language. Oral language remains primary even in these systems.

For the remainder of this book we will mean alphabetic writing systems when we talk about written language. What we say will also apply, for the most part, to languages that are written via symbols for syllables rather than phonemes (individual speech sounds), since syllables are units of sound. Most languages that have writing systems keyed more directly to meaning rather than sound also use some symbols that signal words in the oral language. Nonetheless, for this book, we will restrict ourselves to alphabets when we talk about written language.

When we discuss learning later, we will point out that the best predictor of a child's success in school, including learning to read, is the child's oral vocabulary around the age of five (Dickinson & Neuman 2006; Gee 2004; Hart & Risely 1995). Oral language development is the foundation for success in school and in school-based literacy.

We have already mentioned that a person with a tool (e.g. a hammer, gun, fork-lift, frying pan) is often more powerful than one without a tool. Literacy is a tool, but it is a special tool. It is a tool for delivering oral language. Oral language plus literacy is a different thing than language without literacy, just as a human with a gun is a different thing than a human without a gun. When humans put their legs in a car they can go many places that they cannot go using their legs alone. So, too, when humans combine language with literacy they can do things and "go places" they could not with just language itself.

Here is one example. Before literacy, language was used in "oral cultures," that is, cultures without literacy or with very little literacy (Havelock 1976, 1986; Ong 1982). People used language in oral cultures to retain and pass down memories. This was pretty much the only way they could do it, so they used oral language a good deal for memory purposes. Ultimately they developed special uses of language for memory and the transmission of learning. For instance, oral cultures developed epic stories (like Homer's *Iliad* and *Odyssey*) that preserved the culture's history and knowledge and passed them down through the generations by repeated retellings. Homeric Greek was particularly suited for such stories in the sense that it developed structures and forms (e.g. formulaic phrases, poetic phrasing, and repetitions that enhanced memory and set narrative devices) that aided recollection and retelling (Parry 1971). This is a good example of culture changing, enhancing, and developing language beyond its original forms.

When Greece developed literacy, after Homer's time, human memory could be enhanced in a whole new way. Literacy was a special tool indeed when it came to memory. Now memories (history and knowledge) could be stored (physically) in books and not minds. History and knowledge could be passed down by reading and not talking. Furthermore, knowledge could now be divided into discrete silos or categories like philosophy, diplomacy, biology, cooking, warfare, and so forth. In an oral culture, all knowledge or a good deal of it had to be integrated and stored together in the same highly memorable stories. Separating it into different categories would have meant knowledge had to be memorized in too many different heads and passed down in too many different channels and in non-highly memorable forms like the oral equivalent of an encyclopedia entry.

In a literate culture, oral language has enhanced old capacities and some new ones. For example, when I report an experience to a friend, I can write it down when it is fresh and report it based on what I wrote. I can also check the accuracy of what I said by re-reading the text. The old skill of memory reporting, even when memories are being reported orally, is greatly enhanced.

Language also gains new capabilities when literacy arises. In an oral culture, as we have said, it was too memory-intensive to store every different type or branch of knowledge separately. Indeed, it was hard to create and develop different types and branches of knowledge, since there were grave limits on human memory and the ability of humans to put everything into, and remember everything from, (oral) language that vanished the moment it was spoken.

Once a culture has literacy, however, it can develop different branches of knowledge separately and deeply, well past what any one person could remember or recount. It can also begin to create different styles of language for different branches of knowledge, for example, language for mathematics, language for biology, language for carpentry, language for military affairs, and so forth. Now language has an important property: people can speak (and write) in different varieties of language associated with different branches of knowledge. This skill, however, would soon disappear if we lost all literacy, since, once again, all knowledge would have to be stored in heads and passed down orally.

Language in oral cultures was already multiple. There were different varieties: for example, ritual language, oral epic stories, everyday language, and sometimes, different varieties of language for men and women. But the multiplicity of language has been greatly enhanced by literacy.

Literacy, in respect to memory (retaining memories and passing them down) and to multiplicity (multiple styles of speaking and writing), was a new tool that allowed language to be "leveled up," enhanced for some purposes. In turn, the human mind and human activity were enhanced as well.

As we said before, with tools and technologies there are always both gains and losses. When people change language to do new things, as they did and do with literacy, some old capacities get lost, change radically, or lessen in importance. Thus, the skill of constructing epic stories for passing down history and memories is greatly attenuated in modern literate cultures. We have lost a good deal of the art of using, and many of the language devices for telling, epic oral stories; devices like formulaic phrases, repetition and poetic devices, and dramatic narrative devices.

These skills and devices are still found in many people and cultures, but they are largely attenuated or weakened. We still find them in poetry, but they have nothing like the robust and central place they had in oral cultures when language comported with the likes of Homer.

People at the transition between an oral culture and a literate one (a transition which is normally relatively slow and uneven) can sense the loss of the old ways with words. Today few of us are even aware of the loss of epic oral storytelling as a way of passing down knowledge and binding a culture together. On the other hand, we are acutely aware of some losses caused by digital media since digital media are newer, the losses are more recent, and we stand at the transition between literate culture and digital culture (with literacy located in a new ecology of practices).

This theme of loss looms large when people discuss technology. We often focus on what is lost (e.g. family dinners and dinnertime conversations in the face of television). But there are gains as well, and we need to discuss losses and gains in relationship to each other and in relationship to how losses may be compensated in other quarters. We will return to this theme several times in this book.

When language is regularly delivered by writing in a culture there are not just gains and losses in terms of how we use language. There are also gains and losses for other aspects of the culture and how people act and interact in it, because language is central to what humans do in society and culture.

For example, writing in many societies changes the whole nature of contracts (Graff 1979, 1987). In an oral culture, people have to trust each other's word. If they seek justice in some sort of court, the evidence is primarily based on people's words and how trustworthy those people are or appear to be. With writing, trust is often placed in documents and institutions like law and lawyers, not people's words. Oral evidence is often checked by written evidence. In modern societies, oral language has lost some of its role in creating trust and making contracts.

Literacy as technology

Literacy is a technology, just like cars, tapes and tape recorders, televisions, and digital cameras. Like other technologies, it exists to help us do work that was done without the technology, but less efficiently or less well (or, at least, differently). It also allows people to do new things. Like cars, literacy has remade the world.

As a technology literacy has changed over time. It started as inscriptions made by the human hand with a writing implement. Later humans used printing presses, typewriters, and computers to write with. Today, there are technologies that allow speech to be made directly into print. No need for typing. Quite likely in the future, people will speak into computers in order to write documents and listeners will have the choice to read a document or just have the computer read it out loud. This sort of technology shows clearly that writing is a device for conveying oral (thought, sign) language.

However, this new technology is different from print as we now know it. When we write (compose a written piece) we usually move from silent language in our heads to writing. We do not usually say out loud what we want to write. We just write it. The new technology moves from silent language in our heads to spoken language to writing. Composition will be different—there will be gains and losses. The "old" way of composing will survive, but in a changed ecology. Voicing for the computer what we, silently in our heads, have decided to write will certainly change the composition process. It may make it better in some ways (hearing what we want to say may make us revise it) and worse in others (people may compose "off the top of their heads" by just talking away without much forethought).

Our concern in this book is with literacy as we currently know it best. It is with written language in books, signs, letters, and documents, as well as in ads and alongside images in so-called "multimodal texts" (where images and words are both present). Today, many people tend to view this technology (literacy) as old, traditional, and nowhere near as trendy as newer, often digital, technologies like social media, video games, and digital photography and movies.

Many people also fear that reading and writing are "dying" in the face of new digital media. What they really fear is not that reading and writing are actually dying, but that some of our previously favored ways of reading and writing are dying or becoming much less prevalent (for example, reading a novel quietly by oneself). Reading and writing are, if anything, increasing in the digital world, but they are also changing.

Our argument is that literacy, as a technology for delivering language, in many ways enhanced and empowered language ("leveled up" and "powered up" language to use video-game speak). It gave language new skills (properties, powers) and enhanced old ones. It also attenuated some of language's capacities or changed where, how, why, and when they are applied or used. We will make a similar argument about today's digital media. They too "level up" or "power up" language, with losses and gains, but more gains than losses.

There is, we would argue, a "human nature" and a "language nature" (a basic core form of human language) that was set in motion by evolution. Human nature is what all humans, regardless of culture, share. Language nature is what all languages, regardless of culture, share. Culture has allowed humans and language to develop well beyond their "natures," but their natures still define part (but only part) of what they are, can do, and can be. Culture can lead to developments that so violate the nature of humans (as humans) and language (as language) that they are dangerous and bad for us.

It is not popular today in the social sciences to talk about human nature or language nature. The modern social sciences tend to stress and value cultural variety over what humans and languages share, but they do share important qualities. While their "natures" are very flexible and capable of great modification, they can be violated or broken.

There are specific literacy practices that have violated human nature and language nature. For example, there was a time (which still continues in some places, sadly) when deaf children in the United States where punished for signing and denied the opportunity to learn American Sign Language. This was done in the service of teaching them oral English (which is hard for them, since, of course, they cannot hear) and English literacy, when it is easier to learn English literacy if one has a native language, and a sign language is often the only native language a deaf (from birth) person can acquire.

Humans by nature want and need to express themselves through language. This policy with deaf children violates that nature. Language by nature is interactive and a deaf person can often engage in linguistic interaction a lot better through signing than speaking. The policy also violates the nature of language.

Literacy in modern societies has often so restricted who can publicly express themselves, who can publish and who cannot, and who can produce knowledge and who can only consume it, that the deep desire humans have to express themselves, produce and not just consume, and to be vital parts of and contributors to their societies is often stunted or frustrated. Digital media, today, as we will see, are correcting this deep problem in some important ways.

Effects of literacy

Much has been written about literacy and its effects on a society (Gee 2007a; Goody & Watt 1963; Graff 1979, 1987; Olson 1996; Scribner & Cole 1981; Street 1984). People have claimed that literacy leads to more humane and more modern societies and smarter people. In reality, literacy has had quite different effects on different societies. It has no one set of predictable outcomes. It has certain "affordances," effects that arise if the context is right. Otherwise, literacy's effects, like those of other technologies such as television and computers, depend on the specific contexts in which different literacy practices occur.

The effects of literacy depend on what people actually do with it. In some cases, more literate and educated people are more politically quiescent and accepting of the status quo (because they tend to benefit from the status quo). In other cases, people have used their literacy skills to challenge the status quo and engage in political activism. The same is true of digital media and other technologies. Literacy and digital media can be tools for duping people, controlling them, or supervising them or they can be tools for informing people, liberating them, and giving them a sense of control and self-worth.

In this book we focus both on literacy practices (what people do with others using literacy and other tools and technologies) and the "affordances" of literacy; that is, what literacy tends to lead to, all things being equal, and when other factors do not countermand these affordances. Literacy has affordances in the way a hammer does. A hammer is designed to be useful and good at certain things, but there is no guarantee it will be used in those ways. There also are novel and unexpected uses for hammers. So, too, with literacy. So, too, with digital media.

4

LANGUAGE AND INTERACTION

The bonding–distancing and the content–social interaction continua of language

Consider the two texts below. The first is from a 15-year-old fan fiction writer communicating on the Internet with her fans (Gee & Hayes 2010: 135). The second is from a high school science textbook (Martin 1990: 93):

> I can FINALLY edit my pictures! My cover 4 LH 1.7 looks SICK! I am sooo excited to release it!!!! Check bac 4 it! Should b out either this weekend or next!

> The destruction of a land surface by the combined effects of abrasion and removal of weathered material by transporting agents is called erosion.

These texts represent two poles of language (Levinson 1983; Milroy & Milroy 1985; Tannen 1985). The first is informal and socially bonding language. The second is formal and distancing language. We need to be clear here what "distancing" means. Such academic language is not necessarily distancing to scientists who use it to get their work done. But it is distancing to people not familiar with it. And, more important, it is distancing in the sense that it is designed to be "rational" and not emotional. It is designed to be effective for argumentation and not to project emotion within socially bonding relationships (Bazerman 1988; Myers 1990).

The two examples above are both written texts, though many people (perhaps because of school) associate writing more with the second sort of example than the first. The same poles exist in speech. Compare "It is really nice out today, isn't it?" with "The weather today is well within statistical norms for this season."

The informal/bonding–formal/distancing poles are poles of a continuum. We can use language that lies between these poles. Nonetheless, these poles are an important property of human languages in the world. They are also quickly changing under the influence of digital media in ways we will discuss later.

Many educated people tend to think about language as a tool for exchanging information. They tend to stress the content of what is said over the social relationship that is communicated as well. Yet there is always a social dimension to language, and any use of language lies somewhere on the continuum between informal/bonding language and formal/distance language (Labov 1972).

Language is, and always has been, both a social tool and an information tool. Speakers construct their utterances with an eye both on content (information) and on social relationships. When we use more formal distancing language as opposed to more informal bonding language it implies something about our relationship to the people with whom we are communicating.

Content and social interaction are also on a continuum. In some talk, content is (or appears to be) more important than the social interaction. This language tends to be more formal and distancing. For example, this is often true of a classroom lecture, though social interaction is important here too. Professors usually want to make sure students are awake and alert. In other talk, the social interaction is more important than the content, such as when we talk about the weather to be cordial and friendly to our next-door neighbor. In yet other cases, the importance of content and social interaction are more balanced.

When, in talk, content is much less important than social interaction, we tend to think that the content is "trivial" or "meaningless." Sometimes we call such talk "small talk." However, the point of such talk is not to convey information, but to build or sustain particular kinds of social interaction and relationships, which can be just as important (Gumperz 1982a, 1982b).

We always construct our utterances both to say "something" and to shape a social relationship with our interlocutor. Consider the following utterances. Each one communicates similar content, but expresses different sorts of social relationships with and attitudes toward the person to whom we are speaking:

1 I will be at your party tonight.
2 Can't wait till the party tonight.
3 Let's party hard tonight, bro.
4 I guess I've got to go to your party tonight.
5 It is my privilege to attend your party tonight.
6 If you really want me, I will come to your party tonight.
7 You're lucky I am coming to your party tonight.

These utterances all convey that I will be at the party, though they communicate different things as well. Each utterance also conveys something about the relationship I have with the listener and the attitude I have toward the listener. There is no "neutral" way to communicate. Being neutral or non-committal is just another type of relationship and attitude.

When we study communication in language, we always have to ask what is being said and how it is being said to express a particular type of social relationship and set of attitudes toward that relationship (Gumperz 1982a, 1982b). To coin a few new terms: we have to ask where a particular utterance is on a continuum from "small talk" (where the social interaction/relationship is more important than the content) to "middle talk" (where the social interaction/relationship and content are of more equal importance) to "big talk" (where the content is more important than the social interaction/relationship).

It is important to realize that "small talk" is not always trivial and "big talk" is not always important. Chit-chat before a business meeting about the weather or people's flights to the meeting can be a way for business people to get a sense of each other's personalities and their attitudes toward each other. It can be "hidden work."

On the other hand, many a college lecture, as full of information as it might be, isn't important to either the professor (who wants to go home and write) or the students (who want to go home and socialize). We cannot tell whether a given form of talk is trivial or significant unless we understand the full context in which the talk occurs.

In one sense there are really no trivial interactions for humans. Even the most mundane small talk "greases" social interactions and relationships and sustains them. Even lectures that no one cares about are connected to certificates (degrees) and salaries people do care about. Talk is about achieving purposes and goals that are not always what they seem.

Literacy and the content–social interaction continuum

We said earlier that writing is a delivery system for oral language. It is a delivery system in which spoken words and face-to-face interaction disappear. It is easy to assume that writing conveys just the content, not social relationships and attitudes as oral language does. But this is not true.

The content–social interaction continuum exists for writing just as it does for speech. It must, since writing delivers oral language and oral language is designed to simultaneously communicate content and express social relationships and attitudes. These purposes cannot be separated in human language.

Letters (when they were common) often were used for small talk, though they could also be used for big talk (as when a wife tells her soldier husband that she is pregnant). Many popular magazines are devoted to celebrity gossip (often not even true), a form of small talk. More interestingly, written texts express attitudes and relationships toward their readers, but in different ways than face-to-face talk does.

Writing allows what we will call "fictional relationships" (Scollon & Scollon 1981). In writing, the "person" who communicates and the "people" being communicated to can, at times, both be fictions. This is much harder to accomplish in speech. In speech, fictional relationships often require deception of a sort that in some cases can lead to a jail term.

When the writer (the "speaker" in writing) and the reader (the "listener" in writing) are fictional, interesting things can happen in the social dimension of language. While we tend to think that content is paramount in writing, writing as a technology allows for changes (from face-to-face communication) in how social interaction and relationships, as well as content, are handled.

Consider the warning on a bottle of medicine (Gee 2010):

> Keep this and all drugs out of the reach of children. In case of accidental overdose, seek professional assistance or contact a poison control center immediately. As with any drug, if you are pregnant or nursing a baby, seek the advice of a health professional before using this product.

This warning was probably produced by a team of lawyers and business people. Who is the author of the warning? Who is "speaking"? The business that produces the medicine? A committee? The law? No one individual or institution is the author or writer.

Who is the warning addressed to? Not to us as individuals, and maybe not directly to users of the medicine at all, since many of us don't read the small print on such bottles. Perhaps it is meant to address lawyers or courts if a legal action arises, or, perhaps, it is meant to address "consumers" in either an economic or legal sense.

In regard to the warning, we see that the author (writer) and reader are rather vague or unspecified. We will call them "fictions" (though, in this case, we could just as well call them "abstractions"). What we mean by calling them "fictions" is that we treat the warning as if it were addressed by someone to someone, when it is not really clear who these "someones" actually are.

However, the warning as a piece of institutionalized language still has a "voice" and an "attitude" and creates a certain sort of relationship with the reader, however vague or unclear the intended reader is. This label sounds official but caring. It is much like a homily on drugs, not a direct statement about aspirin. It assumes the reader is knowledgeable, since it assumes one knows how to seek professional assistance, find poison control, and knows what a health professional is. Finally, it seems to assume the reader is a woman.

On more recent aspirin bottle labels, the following was added to the warning above (Gee 2010):

> Children and teenagers should not use this medication for chicken pox or flu symptoms before a doctor is consulted about Reye Syndrome, a rare but serious illness reported to be associated with aspirin. IT IS ESPECIALLY IMPORTANT NOT TO USE ASPIRIN DURING THE LAST 3 MONTHS OF PREGNANCY UNLESS SPECIFICALLY DIRECTED TO DO SO BY A DOCTOR BECAUSE IT MAY CAUSE PROBLEMS IN THE UNBORN CHILD OR COMPLICATIONS DURING DELIVERY.

The instructions are now much more direct, using specific terms such as "children and teenagers," "this medication," "chicken pox or flu," "doctor," "Reye Syndrome," "aspirin," and "pregnancy," rather than "all drugs," "any drug" and vague "health professionals." This is a more authoritarian voice and more intimidating. The reader is directed to care for and protect their children. The message assumes that the reader does not already know all this, while the earlier warning treated its content as common sense.

The warning on the aspirin bottle, as writing, is a way to deliver oral language. It "speaks" and someone listens (reads). But what this written warning does could not be achieved in speech. Abstractions or fictions cannot, in reality, talk and they cannot listen. Writing gives rise to a whole host of new voices, new speakers, and new listeners.

Another example of authors and readers as fictions or abstractions is the essay. The essay is a written form (or genre) that arose in the seventeenth century (Bazerman 1988). By the twentieth century it had become the major written language form used in school, especially in the higher levels of school (high school and college). Being able to write and read essays was taken as a sign of a cultured and educated person. It was a major gateway to obtaining a "good education" and graduating from college. Currently, however, essays do not play the same role and we will discuss this more fully later.

Essays were so central to our twentieth century idea of an educated person that the form of literacy central to schooling has been called "essayist literacy" (Scollon & Scollon 1981). Expository writing and scientific writing are forms of essayist literacy in this broad sense of "essay."

Who is the author of an essay? It would seem that if Joe Doe wrote the essay, Joe Doe is the author. But essays are not supposed to be written with any specific identity or voice connected to Joe as a unique individual. They must be written with the "voice of reason" by the "rational person," unswayed by passion, self-interest, or idiosyncratic properties, using rational argument alone. Furthermore, the essay is not supposed to reflect the specific culture of the author, but the arguments of a rational and, thus, universal mind.

Who is the reader of an essay? It is not really Sally Doe, at least as Sally Doe herself. The essay is addressed to the same sort of person who is supposed to be its author: a rational, universal, acultural, unemotional intellect focused on argument and evidence.

With essays the writer and reader are fictions or abstractions. Real writers and real readers have to write and read as if they were universal, rational, acultural, unemotionally invested, unembodied minds. This was never really possible in reality, but it certainly was a stance authors and readers had to adopt if they wanted to be seen as educated.

There is something good about the essayist's stance: surely we can applaud when people try to rise above self-interest, cultural conflict, and emotional involvement to find common ground. But there is something bad as well: people do not exist without culture, self-interest can often be cloaked in seemingly rational and neutral language, and emotion is not really the opposite of reason but often required for its application (it is hard to write about what you do not care about).

Our goal is not to judge the essay, since it is, to a certain extent, dying as the litmus test of the educated person. What we want to stress is that the creation of author and reader as fictions (universal, rational, acultural beings) is a way of using language tied to the written form of the essay. This way of using language has historically created and influenced new ways of talking and thinking as well. When a student gives a science report to a classroom or a scientist gives a talk at a conference, the "voice" is the same: the reasoning, unself-interested, unemotional, acultural mind.

As an example, consider the sentences below (Gee 2004, 2010):

1   Hornworms sure vary a lot in how well they grow.
2   Hornworm growth exhibits a significant amount of variation.
3   Hornworm growth sure exhibits a significant amount of variation.

Sentence 1 represents what we could call "everyday language," what linguists call "the vernacular." It is the kind of language that can be spoken and written, but it is not likely to appear in an essay or a scientific report. Sentence 2 represents a variety of language that we associate with university professors and other scholars. Such language is sometimes called "academic language" (Schleppegrell 2004). This type of language can be spoken or written, but we associate it more with essayist or expository prose than with speech, especially not with "everyday language."

Sentence 3 is interesting. There is something wrong with it; it sounds "odd" or even humorous. It is not the sort of language we expect to hear or read. Why? Academic language such as in sentence 2—a variety of essayist literacy—is supposed to be written (or spoken) from the voice of reason and argument. "Sure" is an adverb that shows emotional involvement; it shows the speaker (or writer) is impressed or cares. Such emotion is not supposed to be mixed into the academic language in sentence 2.

A different sort of person utters sentence 1 (which we associate more with speech) than writes sentence 2 (which we associate more with academic writing). The person who utters sentence 1 is an emotionally involved person speaking as an everyday person and stating his or her views about hornworms based on what he or she has seen and done. The person who writes sentence 2 is a rational, argument-oriented person speaking as a specialist, stating not his or her own personal views, but the viewpoint of a field or discipline based on scientific evidence (like statistical tests of significance) developed by that field or discipline.

Literacy (written language) gave rise to many other fictional authors and readers. Who authors an ad? The ad agency? The business that paid for it? Whom is it addressing? Consumers? A certain demographic (e.g. young professionals under 40)? Anyone with money?

Who authors a political speech? The politician who gave it? The speech-writer who wrote it? The political party line that dictates what it must contain? Whom is it addressing? Voters? Fellow party members? Swing voters? Citizens?

Oral cultures certainly could have one person speak for another. A shaman or a priest might claim to speak for God in God's words. A councilor might speak for a chief or the king. But it was clear that a particular person was speaking. It was clear that people as fellow members of a shared culture were being addressed. But a written document issued by the United States Catholic bishops is authored by an institution ("the US Church") and addressed to the "laity," that is, an abstract group of people defined by their relationship to that institution. Literacy's proliferation of fictional authors and readers gave rise to a proliferation of institutions and to institutions as themselves actors and "speakers."

The origins of authors and readers as fictions

The origin of authors and readers as fictions, developed so extensively by literacy, resides in the long human past when we first learned to lie (Smith 2007). What would it be like to be a human-like creature that could not tell a lie? Lying may have even led to the expansion of the human brain (Byrne & Whiten 1988). Liars gain a massive advantage in society; other people have to get smarter to catch them and then liars have to get smarter to lie better.

With lying, people could in conversation claim to be something other than they really were. This would not work in a small village, but it will certainly work in a bigger town or city. A person can pretend to be a shaman when he is not, to speak for God when he doesn't, to be an expert when he is not, or to be single when he is married. Jane Austen's novels are replete with women who have to figure out whether the marriageable men they meet are who they claim to be in terms of rank, wealth, and moral character.

Lying and metaphor are closely related. In metaphor we take one thing to be another. When I say that Sue is a "real soldier" or "soldiered on" because she worked so hard through difficulties, I am treating Sue, who is not really a soldier, as if she were a soldier. Metaphors are fictions and in most cases we know it and do not take them literally.

When the United States legal system treats a corporation as a "person" with rights, this is based on a metaphor and is a fiction. A corporation is not really a person. But once this metaphor becomes the law, and society treats corporations as people (for example, says they have "free speech rights" and, thus, can make financial donations to politicians of their choice just like any "other" person), then we can wonder whether it really is a fiction. Have we been deceived by a metaphor that we take too seriously or has the law made a fiction a reality? It is very hard to say.

Literacy allows all sorts of fictional actors to act in ways that have impacts on the world that we don't expect fictions to have. Lying and metaphor were, of course, possible in an oral culture, but literacy allows them to be taken much further.

It is common in modern society to treat institutions as actors who can communicate. We are used to "hearing from" and "talking to" the phone company, the bank, the school, governments, Greenpeace, or media outlets like CNN. We hear from and speak to these institutions in speech and writing, but writing enabled them to arise, grow, and communicate in the first place.

Institutions like a state government, the US Catholic Church, Microsoft Corporation, and Harvard University could not exist without literacy. Writing allows institutions to organize people across time and space, to communicate at a distance, and to set up fictional authors and readers that make the institution an actor and the people to whom it communicates functionaries of the institution.

Bonding and distance

We have been discussing one continuum in talk: (talk as) content versus (talk as) social interaction. Let us return to the related continuum we discussed at the outset of this chapter: talking to achieve social solidarity and bonding with others versus talking in ways that express more social distance and less solidarity and bonding. This is, of course, a divide relevant to the social interaction side of talk. However, it affects the content side, not so much in what we say, but in how we say it, for example, informally or more formally, and how we establish our authority in relation to the content.

When we talk to someone, we can talk in ways that express (or seek to achieve) closeness, solidarity, and bonding with them. We can also talk in ways that express (or seek to achieve) more social distance and less closeness and bonding. We may express such distance because we want to express respect and deference to a listener we assume to be higher in status than ourselves. We may express such distance because we see the listener as lower in status than ourselves (as, for example, happens sometimes when some people are talking to service workers). Finally, we may express such distance because we do not know the listener well—the listener is a stranger.

There are basically four types of talk from this social point of view. We can talk to one another as intimates. Let's call this intimate talk. This is how spouses, parents and children, and close friends often talk with each other. We can talk to one another as peers; by a "peer" we mean not a close friend, but an equal whom we know but with whom we are not intimate (or do not wish at the time to treat as an intimate; for example, when talking to one's spouse in a shared workplace). Let's call this peer talk. We can talk to another person in ways that indicate he or she is higher status or lower status than we are. Let's call this status talk and further divide status talk into "up-status talk" (to a person of higher status or whom we want to treat as higher status) and "down-status talk" (to a person of lower status or whom we want to treat as lower in status). Finally, there is talk between strangers—and different cultures have quite different rules about how to treat strangers. Let's call this stranger talk.

Intimate talk is usually highly informal. Up-status talk is usually highly or at least fairly formal. Peer talk is somewhere in-between. These features of different kinds of social talk are true across many cultures and cultural groups. How people talk when they are engaged in down-status talk and stranger talk is more variable across cultures. In some cultures, people don't talk to strangers at all, in others they do. In some cultures people talk very respectfully to strangers, in some they talk to them like peers, and in others they are ruder. And, of course, talk varies by how we assess the stranger (for example, in terms of social class). The same is true of down-status talk, which can be respectful, fairly formal, peer-like, or informal—and sometimes brusque and rude.

There is such variability around down-status talk and stranger talk because all languages and cultures have distinctive ways to show politeness or withhold it. Politeness is a core property of language (Brown & Levinson 1987; Levinson 1983). When we speak we must choose how polite to be. In almost all cultures, people do not engage in elaborate politeness with intimates or peers. With intimates, dropping markers of politeness can be a sign of bonding and intimacy. With peers, a modicum of politeness is usually required, though not elaborate politeness. In talking to higher status people, more or less elaborate politeness is usually required. Of course, different cultures and different languages show politeness in different ways.

In talking to strangers and lower status people, cultures differ in how much or little politeness to apply. This is because they differ on how they view things like being a stranger (i.e. an "outsider") or being low in status. In some instances and societies, strangers and lower status people are, in a sense, "less human." In other instances and societies, they are not.

The trouble with strangers and people whom we think are lower in status is that we often care somewhat less how they feel and respond to us because we do not think any important consequences will arise. The stranger we may never see again and the lower status person may have less power. In a sense, we can—but this does not mean we do—take such people for granted. With peers and people higher in status we worry about their responses and must not take them for granted.

Oddly enough, intimates are people whom we often take for granted as well (Wolfson 1989). We assume they will excuse, ignore, or forgive our lapses in behavior. We often feel we don't need to worry too much about how they react to what we say and do, either because we think we know their feelings and reactions pretty thoroughly (and take for granted they won't change) or we have become so comfortable with them that we do not any longer reflect on their responses. For this reason humans sometimes treat strangers and intimates less respectfully and carefully—because they take them for granted—than they do peers and people higher in status, whose feelings and reactions they have to monitor and worry about. We are often at "our best" or "on our best behavior" with peers and higher status people.

Writing created a dilemma around the social and politeness aspects of oral language. Some forms of writing, most especially essayist writing, are written to "strangers." As writers of such prose we are supposed to write for a generalized rational reader, not specific people we know. How do we treat such a reader? This is, in fact, a cultural dilemma for some people. Some Native American groups, for instance, tend not to talk to people they do not know, because they avoid intervening in other people's affairs or otherwise imposing on people unless they have "permission" to do so (Scollon & Scollon 1981). They expect the same respect for themselves. They only want to communicate when they know enough about the person to whom they are communicating to make their communication relevant and to predict how their communication will be received. Since an essay requires them to communicate with people whom they do not know, it is a form of communication they would reject.

There are also situations in our society when people who are speaking or writing to peers or other known people are supposed to ignore the fact that they know these people and share a good deal of background knowledge with them. For example, when students write essays for teachers, they are expected to write as if they do not know what the teacher already knows and doesn't. A student giving an oral report on a science project to his or her classmates is supposed to pretend they are not all peers who share a lot of knowledge (e.g. they may even have done the same project), but "strangers" who need to be told everything explicitly and relatively formally.

We are in the realm of fiction again—our peers, for example, have become strangers—which is what we expect from writing. Notice that writing gives rise to these sorts of fictional "speakers" and "listeners" in both written texts and oral ones. A written or oral science report in school is still given from the voice of a rational expert (when the student may be no such thing).

One kind of fiction that writing readily allows is anonymity. Authors can easily pretend to be someone else or hide their true identities. A woman can write a novel under the name of a man or vice versa. A debt consolidation company can send out a letter that looks like it is from a government agency. An oil company lobbyist can write an editorial for a local newspaper claiming to be an environmentalist. Authors can, even if they use their own names, enact personalities: for example, say rude and hateful things about their political opponents, women, or some racial group, that they would never dream of saying face-to-face. Flaming did not arise with the Internet. Worries about what communications and writers are trustworthy did not arise with the Internet. They arose with lies and misplaced metaphors long ago in the history of oral language. But they became major concerns with the rise of literacy.

Problems with and dilemmas over strangers, intimacy, status, fictions, lying, metaphors, anonymity, and institutions are inherent in literacy. They become yet more complex with the rise of digital media. Digital media are transforming the content–social poles of language and the ways in which we combine information and interaction. Digital media are also transforming the solidarity–distance poles and the ways in which we express and enact relationships in language.

5

NEW KINDS OF PEOPLE AND RELATIONSHIPS

Strangers

In the previous chapter, we introduced the idea that one function of language is to communicate social bonding versus social distance. In this chapter, we will expand on this idea and consider how digital media are changing our social relationships, particularly whom we consider to be strangers and intimates.

In the last chapter we saw that strangers are one problem that nearly all cultures face. In a small village or in a small band of hunters and gatherers, there were usually no strangers, so there was no problem with how to interact with them. But in more complex social groups there are strangers. How should we speak to them?

Cultures, and even individuals within larger cultures and societies, differ in how they choose to talk to strangers (Brown & Levinson 1987; Levinson 1983; Scollon & Scollon 1981; Wolfson 1989). Think about what you would do if you were standing next to a stranger at a bus stop for some time. Some people will talk to the stranger and use informal, friendly language near the bonding end of the bonding–distance continuum. They do this, perhaps, to show the stranger that they do not represent a threat. A potential problem is that the stranger may either not want to treat the speaker in such an informal and friendly way or, on the other hand, may take the bonding too seriously and think that the speaker really means more friendship than he or she actually intends. The speaker may only be using "small talk" socially to lubricate a potentially uncomfortable situation.

Other people choose either more formal, polite, distancing language or choose to stay silent and not talk at all to the stranger. In this case, a potential problem is that the stranger may feel threatened if not addressed at all or may resent being addressed, or may be offended by formal, distancing talk, expecting a more friendly overture. That's the trouble with strangers. We do not know the social "rules" they expect to be followed and they do not necessarily share the "rules" by which we operate.

Part of what complicates matters is that people across and sometimes within cultures differ in how they wished to be treated (Brown & Levinson 1987). Some people have a stronger need for acceptance and bonding than others. They feel insulted if left out and not included. Such people are said, by sociologists, to have stronger "positive face needs" than "negative face needs."

Other people have a stronger need for not being imposed upon than others. They feel insulted or bothered if people interact with them or make requests of them, or otherwise attempt to include them, without their explicit permission or without knowing them well. Sociologists say such people have stronger "negative face needs" than "positive face needs."

Everyone has both bonding needs and needs to be respected and not to be imposed upon. All people have both positive (a need to be included and involved) and negative (a need to be left alone and not imposed upon) face needs. But people differ in which of these needs are stronger for them or stronger for them in different contexts.

The problem with strangers is more complex in modern urban societies where many different sorts of people are in close proximity. We can be too polite (distant) when people expect us to be friendlier. We can be too friendly when people expect us to be more polite and distant. We can talk when they do not want or expect us to talk. There are many opportunities for insulting people. The problem with strangers becomes yet more complex with digital media.

Strong and weak ties

We have, what have been called, "strong ties" to people we know well, because we see and relate to them often. We have, what have been called, "weak ties" to people whom we do not know well, because we do not see and relate to them often (Easley & Kleinberg 2010; Granovetter 1973; Lin 2001).

There are good and bad aspects of both strong and weak ties. The people to whom we have strong ties are more likely to give us help and support when we need it. That is a good thing about them. The "bad" thing is that these are people with whom we share a good deal of knowledge and background. Such people are not often a source of truly new and rare information for us.

The people with whom we have weak ties are not close to us and not likely to "be there" for us if we need them. They owe us nothing. That is the bad part. However, these are people with whom we share much less knowledge and background. Such people are much more likely to know something we do not already know and give us new or rare information. That is the good part.

Consider a working-class man who lost his job in a bad economy. The people with whom he has strong ties are unlikely to know about new jobs that he does not already know about. Indeed, many of them may have also lost their jobs. They already will have shared all they know with each other.

However, if this man has weak ties with people he does not know well—that is, if he has some contact with people outside of his normal social network—these people may know about jobs and possibilities he and his friends do not already know about. Perhaps they know about a job in a new field outside the man's neighborhood and can even give the man a name and contact number.

In stable times where change is slow, weak ties are not that important. But in fast-changing and unpredictable times, weak ties are crucial. They may be the only way we can get fast-changing information in order to cope and survive.

For most of human history, people had strong ties with other people much like themselves, people with whom they lived closely and shared a culture. In modern cities, people can and do come to have strong ties with other people from different social and cultural groups, through much interaction and because they live or work near each other.

Digital media have greatly changed the nature of strong and weak ties (Constant *et al.* 1996; Haythornthwaite 2002). They have greatly complicated both the perils and possibilities of strangers. Thanks to digital media, everyone in the digitally connected parts of the world, in a sense, lives next to each other. People can be strangers and intimates at one and the same time. This has never been possible in history before.

Literacy already opened up this possibility. People could have long-term correspondences (via letters) with someone else across the globe. They may never have met in person and they may have known little about each other personally. However, in such cases, writers often shared professional, religious, or class affiliations. The affordances of digital media were necessary to make "intimate strangers" a reality on a large scale.

Strong weak ties and intimate strangers: A world of contradictions

Digital media are, in part, like literacy, a delivery system for language. However, they create conditions in which language has never before been used. For most of human history, people did not have strong ties (interact regularly) with people whom they did not know well or who were, in fact, strangers. They did not expect to get a great deal of new and rare information from their intimates and close friends. At the same time, they did not expect to get help and support from people they did not know well. Now all this has changed.

Let's consider a little story. It's the early days of *World of WarCraft*, a game we will just call *WoW*. *WoW* is an extremely popular massively multiplayer video game. Players team up with other players to engage in quests (e.g. finding things and fighting things). At any one time, on a given server, thousands of real people will be playing the game together. Even if you are not playing directly with other people in a group, you can run into them at any time in the big wide world of *WoW*. What other people do can affect what you do (e.g. what they do may help or hinder you). You can, if you wish, talk to these other people any time you want, and even ask them for help or just socialize with them.

When people play *WoW* they are represented in the game by an avatar, a virtual character that need not bear any physical resemblance to the player. The avatar for a

50-year-old white male may be, for instance, a blue female night elf. When players interact, no one knows who they are, their nation, age, race, or gender, unless they are using voice chat (players often type to each other) or they choose to divulge such information.

WoW is now the most popular massively multiplayer video game in the world. When *WoW* first launched, a player whose avatar was named Allele began to play the game. Like many others, the player-as-Allele played hundreds of hours and became quite adept at the game. He often encountered another player, whose avatar was named Band. They quested together at times and with other people. They often talked, at first knowing nothing about each other except that they were both elves. Eventually they talked about their real identities and what they did in the "real world."

Allele was a white man in his fifties, living in the United States. Band was an Albanian man in his twenties. Allele ran successful technology start-ups in Silicon Valley and Band worked for a struggling technology company in Albania. Allele sent Band some software and gave him technical advice, both of which helped Band's company. Band, in return, bought a very special sword in *WoW* and gave it as a gift to Allele, who used it to gain more power and status in the game.

In one sense, Allele and Band had strong ties. They interacted regularly, came to know a good deal about each other, shared personal information, and used bonding language with each other. Yet they were "strangers" in the sense that they had never seen each other and shared little background and culture.

In another sense, Allele and Band had weak ties. They came from different worlds and often shared new and rare information with each other. Indeed, they were a typical "weak tie" source of such information for each other. Yet they also offered each other the sort of free support and help that we expect only from friends, people to whom we have strong ties.

There is a real paradox or contradiction here. Allele and Band's tie was both strong and weak. They benefited from both strong and weak ties. We can say that they had a "strong weak tie," which sounds like a contradiction—and it is—but a contradiction that happens through digital media all the time all over the world.

The strong weak tie between Allele and Band seems like a good thing. We are more worried when a strong weak tie arises on the Internet between an old man in one place and a teenage girl in another, for example. Like all effects of technology, strong weak ties can be good or bad depending on context and circumstances.

New kinds of relationships? New kinds of people?

The whole idea of who a person is, as well as who is or who is not a stranger or an intimate, is changing thanks to digital media. When two people have interacted in a game like *WoW* as much as Allele and Band, are they friends? Do they really know each other? What is the difference between Allele (a character in the game, but controlled by a human), the fifty-something white male playing Allele (a person in the real world), and that fifty-something white male choosing to communicate and act in certain ways when, and sometimes only when, he is playing as Allele?

Let's turn to another story. Here another fifty-something white man is playing *WoW* with his forty-something wife. They both have attractive (albeit blue) female elf avatars. While they are playing they encounter a male elf character who asks them if they are male or female in "real life." The man replies that they are sisters, one fifteen, one seventeen, playing together. The male elf, who claims to be a teenage boy, starts to flirt with the fifty-something man, eventually offering to play the game with "her" every day.

The man has no idea how to respond to such flirtation. He has never experienced such a thing in real life, having never been an attractive teenage girl. He remembers the power teenage girls seemed to have when he was a teenage boy. He has always wondered about that power and what it felt like to have it. He asked his wife how to respond as a teenage girl and with her help was soon chatting and joking with the boy. He was amazed by the experience of something that was, in a sense, literally impossible.

Of course, the teenage boy could have been an old man or woman or anyone else. This story will seem "creepy" to many readers. The question relevant to our discussion is, though, what does this anecdote tell us about these people as "real" people? Did the man discover something "real" about himself, or about human relationships, whether good or bad? Do such experiences, afforded by digital media, allow us to become "new people" in any sense?

Here is yet another story. *Second Life* is a massively multiplayer virtual world, rather than a game. It is a virtual world that is designed and built by its own players. It contains a great many different environments in which people do everything from creating artwork to working as bartenders to participating in political organizations. Much of what people do involves socializing with each other. In *Second Life* people have avatars, as in *WoW*, and these avatars can look like any sort of human or many non-human creatures.

Our story is about one avatar that became popular in *Second Life* (Au 2008). Many people felt that the person controlling this avatar, whoever he or she "really" was in "real life," was a fascinating, friendly, and good person. Many people wanted to interact with the person and sought the person out.

The "person" controlling the avatar was not one person. It was five patients in a long-term care facility. These were people who had spent their lives in this facility because of severe deformities. A nurse controlled their common avatar and they made decisions together about what the avatar should say and do. These were people who, in the outside world, were feared and shunned. In *Second Life*, they were sought out and valued. They had never before experienced what it was like to be treated as valuable, "normal" people, to be valued for who they were and not what they looked like. They loved playing *Second Life*.

In *Second Life* these people were valued for "who they were" and not what they looked like. But let's think a minute about what that means: they were "themselves," something they could not be in "real life," only when they were a single avatar representing five people! Who was this "one" person (a popular one)? We really are talking about something that has never happened on earth before. For most of human history, one's fate was eternal and there was no second chance at life. But these people have broken, albeit in a small way and only for a moment, the skein of fate. This is, indeed, the stuff of the gods.

Literature

We misled you. We said that the play with identities and relationships we have been discussing was unique to digital media. We said this because, at its current scale and global reach, it is true. But something similar can happen with literature, though the ability of literature to set free new identities eventually was "tamed" by the institution of school. We wonder if the ability of digital media to set free new identities will eventually be tamed by institutions.

Consider what once was called "the canon." The canon was the list of great literature by writers like John Milton, William Shakespeare, and Jane Austen. Today, the very idea of a canon is controversial. Interestingly, both conservatives and liberals agree that canonical literature (the so-called "Great Books") is indoctrinating. The right wing applauds the work the canon can do to align people with what it sees as universal values, values that it sees as already its own. The left wing decries this same thing, claiming that the values embedded in the canon are, far from being universal, just a historically and culturally specific instantiation of the values of certain Western, "middle-class" white people, people who wish to use the canon to enshrine their values and perspectives as superior.

Both views show a woeful ignorance of, and even a certain disdain for, how many people in the past (especially many poor people, people who rarely get invited into academic debates about the canon) actually read and used canonical works like those of Homer, Shakespeare, Milton, Carlyle, Arnold, Austen, Emerson, and a great many others. Many a woman, nonwhite, or poor person actually read canonical works as empowering texts that made them challenge the class hierarchy of their societies and the ways in which schools, churches, and rich people upheld this hierarchy in their own favor.

Jonathan Rose's (2001) massive tome, The *Intellectual Life of the British Working Classes*, is full of stories from the eighteenth through the twentieth century of women, poor people, and nonwhite people who interpreted canonical literature as representing their own values and aspirations and not those of the wealthy and powerful. For example, Mary Smith (b. 1822), a shoemaker's daughter, who stated that: "For long years Englishwomen's souls were almost as sorely crippled and cramped by the devices of the school room, as the Chinese women's feet by their shoes," said this about reading Shakespeare, Dryden, and Goldsmith:

> These authors wrote from their hearts for humanity, and I could follow them
> fully and with delight, though but a child. They awakened my young nature,
> and I found for the first time that my pondering heart was akin to that of

the whole human race. … Carlyle's gospel of Work and exposure of Shams, and his universal onslaught on the nothings and appearances of society, gave strength and life to my vague but true enthusiasm. (Rose 2001: 45)

The left wing may say that Mary Smith was conforming to the dictates of the elites in her society without knowing it and mistakenly taking their values to be her own. But the only people who were duped by the canon were the right-wing elites who thought it uncritically represented their viewpoints and the left wing who agreed with them. Mary Smith interpreted what for us is "high literature" but for her was "popular" literature to say that even the daughter of a shoemaker was the equal, in intelligence and humanity, of any rich person.

Why did Mary Smith read canonical works as affirming her humanity and rights to equality in a hierarchical society? She identified *herself* with the characters and viewpoints in these books. She projected herself into them. She didn't distance herself from the hero because he was a male and a king in a Shakespeare play, however much she might have wanted and certainly deserved female heroes. She saw herself as projected into that powerful monarch. Perhaps sometimes when she read Shakespeare, she was a king and other times a queen. Perhaps sometimes when she read Shakespeare, she was not a traditional monarch at all but a monarch shoe-maker with the dignity and the human worth of a traditional monarch. Perhaps sometimes, she was all these and more. Remember, she was not just taking on the life of a virtual character in the book or play. She was also projecting herself into that character, creating something that both she and Shakespeare made, neither one of them alone.

Neither the right nor the left wing wrote the scripts for the plays in Mary Smith's mind, no matter how influenced she, like all of us, was by the political and cultural factors of her time. Shakespeare was deeply influenced by his own times, but he wrote original scripts nonetheless. So did Mary Smith. Mary Smith read books that today's students find boring, with the excitement that today's students find in video games, because, perhaps, she read them at least in part much like those students sometimes play video games, actively, critically, and projectively; that is, she projected herself into the text so that a king or queen became her "avatar" in the text.

In the end, Mary Smith and many more like her believed that canonical litera-ture, far from representing the values of wealthy elites, undermined their values and showed them for the hypocrites they were. The message Mary Smith got from such literature was that she was at least their equal and in all likelihood their better.

Conservatives and liberals who argue over the canon tend to act as if people like Mary Smith will read such books and either want to emulate their "betters" (the right-wing perspective) or passively accept the inferiority ascribed to them by the elite (the left-wing view). The Mary Smiths of the world need do no such thing. These people already know that they are thinking, worthy beings. They sometimes see in canonical literature examples of who and what they could be, if others in society ceased to disdain them.

Do we think there is some definitive list of "Great Books"? By no means. For us, the canon is and was never a closed list. Any book is canonical if it lends itself to the powerful projective work in which Mary Smith engaged and leads people to desire not more hierarchy, but more opportunities for the display of human worth and the greater development of human capacities for all people. A work is canonical, for us, if it gives people, in Kenneth Burke's (1993: 19) phrase, new and better "equipment for living" in a harsh and unfair world.

In this sense, works like Ralph Ellison's *Invisible Man* and Gloria Naylor's *Mama Day* are canonical for us and many other people. There are a good many books written by women, nonwhite people, and poor people that never got on the "official" canon as a list, due to the workings of racism and patriarchy, but are most certainly, in our terms, canonical.

Traditional canonical works, like those of Homer, Shakespeare, Milton, and Dryden, function today quite differently than they did in Mary Smith's day. Smith's society denied her any sort of schooling that gave her access to these books. In fact, her society felt it inappropriate for a shoemaker's daughter to be reading such books. She picked them up anyway with defiance, and saw in them resonances with herself that just further proved her own intelligence and worth.

Schools, by and large, have tamed the canon. They have made it into the stuff of tests, multiple-choice answers, and standardized responses. Everyone now, finally, has access to the canon at a time when schools have rendered it toothless. Young people today have access to far more texts, images, and diverse media of far more kinds than even the wealthy of Mary's Smith time. Milton's *Paradise Lost* played a very different role in the textual ecology of Smith's world than it does for a young person today. For her it was a precious book, hard won through a great deal of physical labor (to buy it, if she didn't borrow it) and mental labor (to read it seriously). For a young person today, the book is cheap to buy and the school tells them how to read it in the "right" way (or get a poor grade).

This is no plea for reading Milton, though we are sure many people still get a great deal out of traditional canonical literature when they read it of their own choosing, usually outside of school. There is plenty of evidence that people today still read and watch many things that serve some of the same purposes that canonical literature did for Mary Smith (Jenkins 2006b).

Video games are a new form of art. They will not replace books; they will sit beside them, interact with them, and change them and their role in society in various ways, as, indeed, they are already doing with movies. (Today many movies are based on video games and many more are influenced by them.) We have no idea yet how people "read" video games, what meanings they make from them. Still less do we know how they will "read" them in the future. It won't do to start this investigation by assuming they are dupes of capitalist marketers, though of course, some of them very likely are. But there will always be Mary Smiths out there who use cultural products, whether "high" or "low," for good purposes.

6

LITERACY AND INTERPRETATION

Interpretation police

Writing is a delivery system for oral language. Delivery systems, as we have said, are not trivial and they have effects, often significant ones. Cars deliver people. One effect is people walk less and get fatter. Another effect is that they can meet more people in more places than they could without such transportation.

One effect of written language is that it defers negotiation over what things mean away from face-to-face communication to what we might call "interpretation police." In an oral culture, there is no way to decide what people mean other than by listening to them. If we are unsure what they mean, we have to ask them and, perhaps, argue with them.

Even in oral cultures there is the beginning of interpretation police, people who police interpretations or meanings. A shaman, priest, elder, or leader may claim special authority to determine what certain myths, religious claims, or stories "really" mean. But these interpretation police have to explicate this knowledge in speech. They have to work out their claims in public in front of members of the group. They have to face questions.

Writing allows a separation between when and where something is "said" (written) and when and where it is interpreted. It can be written in one place and time and interpreted at another place and time. Further, far beyond what is possible in an oral culture, groups of people can present themselves as "experts" on what certain types of language or certain types of texts mean.

Writing gives rise to a proliferation of types of language (e.g. the language of lawyers, engineers, biologists, doctors, and diplomats) and types of texts (e.g. novels, news reports, scientific papers, technical manuals, and blogs). It also gives rise to a concomitant proliferation of groups of people who "own" certain sorts of language and texts. They claim to know what such language and texts "really" mean. They dispute these meanings among themselves and often feel no real need to defend themselves to the wider community of non-experts. They "police" the texts they "own" and tell other people what the texts really mean.

For example, in the heyday of the so-called "New Criticism" (a form of close reading of literary texts) in university English departments, experts in literary criticism claimed to know, through special competency and training, what a Henry James novel or a Shakespeare play really meant (Ransom 1941; Wimsatt & Beardsley 1946). They policed the interpretation of such texts, dictating which readers were "right" and which were "wrong."

In a world of writing, we take it for granted that lawyers will have the last word on what contracts mean; doctors will have the last word on what medical research means for treatment; a movie critic will have the last word on what a film means and whether it is good. Even the critic's view will get trumped by the word of the film scholar. Oral cultures had experts and specially interpreted forms of language (e.g. religious language), but nothing like the proliferation of expertise and special forms of language that came with writing and most especially with print.

Thus, writing gives rise to many different types of language and different types of texts. It also gives rise to interpretation police, experts who claim to know what certain types of language and texts really mean. These experts need institutions to support them and enforce their power. The literary critic needs the university English department; lawyers need law schools, courts, and legal associations; doctors need medical schools, hospitals, insurance companies, and medical associations; movie critics need media outlets that "canonize" them as experts; and film scholars need film schools, journals, and conferences. Institutions proliferate everywhere and divide the expert from the non-expert "everyday person."

In an oral culture, while some people may have known more about animals and plants, for example, than others, everyone in the culture shared a great deal of knowledge about such things. Even what the more expert people did and said was public and everyone needed to know, of course, what was safe to eat and what was not. Today we eat food with no idea what is in it and we trust experts and bureaucrats when they tell us it is safe (often to our peril, it turns out).

With writing, experts come to function like priests in a religion (Kermode 1979). They tell us what certain sorts of texts mean (e.g. the Bible, Shakespeare, legal contracts, novels), assure us that they see deeper meanings than "everyday" people would ever see, and correct us when we dare try to interpret the texts ourselves (sometimes with threatened punishments, e.g. Hell or a bad grade).

This proliferation of languages and texts, experts and institutions is obviously both good and bad. Life today is less nasty, brutish, and short than it was in oral cultures. Medicine has made great advances and enforcing contracts across wide stretches of space and time is essential for a functioning modern economy. At the same time, experts and institutions have deskilled everyday people, taken away our own need to know and choose for ourselves, and, at times, misled us about how much they really know and how they know it (Douglas 1986).

The crisis of the experts

All major cultural changes, like the advent of literacy, are complex and their effects are multiple, neither all good or all bad. Today the nature and role of experts and the institutions that support them and enforce their expertise are changing. Experts are, in a sense, in crisis (Collins & Evans 2007; Friedman 2005; Gladwell 2008; Shirky 2008, 2010).

Let's take one telling example. As we write this, the United States and much of the rest of the world is in the midst of the largest recession since the Great Depression. This global economic downturn was caused by complex financial practices centered in the United States (Johnson & Kwak 2010; Lewis 2010). These practices allowed mortgage brokers to give loans on houses (a mortgage) to people who, in fact, could not afford them. They sold these mortgages to investment banks, passing on the risk that the person who took out the mortgage would default on payments to the banks. The brokers made their money on fees, not on the mortgage payments (which the bank collected).

The bankers took many of these mortgages and consolidated them into bonds that they sold to investors, who collected the mortgage payments. The banks, too, passed on the risk of defaults to others and made their money primarily from fees for their services. An investor in Iceland might end up owning a mortgage on a house in California as part of many mortgages or pieces of them rolled into the bond he bought. The relationship between the homeowner and the person who owned his or her mortgage was not local, but distributed across a distance and a global world. In order to entice investors to buy mortgages rolled up into bonds, banks encouraged rating agencies to give these bonds a high rating, which meant they were considered safe investments (when they were not). When a great many people defaulted on their home payments, pretty much all at the same time, the whole system collapsed.

The institutions that engaged in these practices (brokerage firms, investment banks, rating agencies, regulators that did not properly regulate) claimed that these practices were too complex and technical for everyday people to understand. We had to trust their expertise as they got rich and eventually "everyday people" got poorer when the economy crashed.

We see here a complex set of relationships among institutions. It is a complex system with many interacting variables, unpredictable consequences, unintended consequences, and high risk for damage and harm. The world is filled with such risky complex systems and their results, like the environment and global warming, the global economy, global population growth, global cultural and religious conflicts, and outcomes of the interrelationships between all of these designed and natural systems (like the heat island effect in cities). Experts tell us they understand these systems much better than we do, but their consequences often become dangerous and then the experts can't explain why.

When the economy collapsed, Alan Greenspan, considered the leading economic expert in the world and long-time head of the Federal Reserve Bank in the United

States, said he had no idea why the collapse happened, never saw it coming, and could not explain it. His expertise had run dry (Andrews 2008). Today, in the face of complex systems, individual expertise is dangerous. Such experts undervalue what they do not know and overvalue what they do.

Understanding and dealing with the consequences of complex systems requires pooling different types of expertise from different domains in a highly collaborative way (Parker 2002). Going it alone is out of date and dangerous. Greenspan needed to collaborate with people who thought about history, human psychology (and greed), cultural changes (including in business), institutional relationships, global economies and politics, and the sociology of human interactions within institutions. Economic theory by itself, especially as Alan Greenspan understood it, was dangerous because it allowed Greenspan to account for too little of the big picture and to trust too much in his own expertise (and to ask everyday people for this same trust).

Greenspan needed to pay attention to what actors, including everyday people, were doing in practice, not just pay attention to them as statistics. This was hard for him to do, in part, because, like many elites, he lived in an isolated world of power and wealth. When we live in isolated worlds, rich or poor, we tend to interact only with people like ourselves and entrench our beliefs. We then proceed to ignore what we do not know or see.

Literacy gave rise to a world of experts and institutions that for a long time did us a world of good (and some bad), but which now is killing us (literally). The world is too complex for this old-fashioned notion of experts. Not only is pooling different sorts of expertise in a collaborative fashion, with new jointly shared language and methods, crucial today. So is the "wisdom" of "everyday people." Today, the "everyday person," so long marginalized as a knower by experts and their institutions, is receiving renewed attention as a resource for solving global problems.

Wisdom of the crowd

There is now a fairly well studied phenomenon known as the "wisdom of the crowd" (Surowiecki 2004). If we ask people how many coins or jelly beans there are in a big jar, each person will answer incorrectly and by a pretty big measure. But if we average the answers across enough people we get very close to the actual number. The "crowd" knows how many coins or beans there are, but no one person as an individual does. There is "wisdom" in the crowd that is not in individual people.

The same phenomenon is apparent in many other cases. A crowd, for example, can estimate the weight of a steer much more accurately than an individual, even an expert. A crowd can pick better-performing stocks or predict the outcomes of a set of sports events (like Sunday's football games) better than can experts. Obtaining the favored answers of a crowd, or some sort of average, often is more useful than asking an expert (though often experts can helpfully interpret or use the crowd's answer by pooling their expertise with the wisdom of the crowd).

There are certain features that a crowd must have if it is to be "wise." First, it must be large and diverse. There must be, in the crowd, a good deal of diversity among people's experiences and accordingly, their knowledge. Second, no one in the crowd should defer to others, assuming that what they know or believe is less credible than what others who seem smarter or more powerful claim to know. Third, people in the crowd must care enough about the answer to make their best effort. Such crowd decision-making situations are sometimes set up as "markets" where people bet on the answer or can win something if they are right.

After 9/11, the United States Department of Defense wanted to set up a wisdom-of-the-crowd market for terrorist attacks (Stossel 2008). People would bet on where the next terrorist attack would happen and be rewarded if they were correct. The experts would consult this information in their anti-terrorism efforts. It was believed this approach would give the experts insights beyond what they could gain on their own. The proposal gave rise to an outcry, since it seemed wrong for people to benefit from being right about an attack on others, but it could have worked.

Another example of wisdom of the crowd being used in highly consequential situations is reading X-rays looking for early tumors that could be cancerous (Thomas Mackie, personal communication; see also Howe 2008b). It turns out that these little lumps are very hard even for experts to find on an X-ray. But if thousands of people looked at them and said where they thought they saw a lump, the crowd's average can, with big enough numbers, converge on a correct answer in many cases, or, at least, tell experts one good place to check.

The wisdom-of-the-crowd approach, or "crowdsourcing" (Howe 2008a), works because one never knows when someone who is not an expert (or, at least, an expert in the relevant field) may know something or have experienced something others do not know or have not experienced. Information is pooled widely. Often experts can be very helpful at assessing the breadth of information in a wisdom-of-the-crowd market and evaluating answers. But it remains true that crowds often converge on better answers than experts, whether they are picking stocks, estimating risks, or betting on games.

Trust and writing

Today expertise and knowledge reside less in the head of an individual expert and increasingly in collaborating groups of experts and everyday people ("the crowd"). The current crisis of expertise is partly about trust, or a lack of trust, in our traditional authority figures. However, literacy started a crisis long ago, or at least a transformation of trust. The seeds of today's crisis were there in the rise of written language.

When someone made a claim in an oral culture, listeners could ask the speaker why they should trust what he or she had said. As in today's face-to-face conversations, such trust was rooted in the speaker's reputation, history, and social standing in the community. Of course, if someone said there was an elephant in his tent, people could simply go check. But sometimes speakers claimed that they had authority from God, ancestors, or sanctioned stories (e.g. myths) passed down through the generations. There was no way, beyond talking to the speaker, or others in the community, to check such claims. Talk was final, unless force intervened to make people stop questioning.

With the advent of writing, the trust question could be answered in a quite different way. The speaker could produce written "evidence," that is, a written document that supported his or her assertions. For example, a person could show a birth certificate as evidence of age and birthplace, or refer to a book written by a Wall Street executive to support claims about unethical financial practices among stockbrokers. But then the question arises about what the written document means and why one should trust it. With literacy, the trust issue is often displaced from the speaker or author to the written text.

The trustworthiness of a written document might be thought to reside in its author. In some cases, the credibility of the author is sufficient, of course. But often the author is not physically present and sometimes long dead. And, as we saw earlier, sometimes authors are fictions or abstractions (e.g. institutions or groups). Since the author is often not available to clarify or vouch for what he or she wrote, someone else has to interpret or verify a written text before we can know whether or not it is trustworthy.

Now another problem arises. Very often, people disagree over what texts mean, especially texts that offer unique or specialist knowledge. As such disagreements arise, someone or something must settle them. Historically, the force that settles disagreements about interpretation is wielded by some sort of interpretation police, that is, experts who claim special knowledge about what special sorts of texts mean. This is what keeps lawyers, judges, academics, and critics in business.

The issue of trust has now been displaced from the speaker or author to the text to the expert. But why should we trust the expert? We have already seen that today there is a crisis of trust in experts. We trust the expert because of the institutions that trained the expert and that support and enforce the expert's expertise. As we have said, literacy is integrally tied to institutions. This is partly so because of trust.

This issue of writing and trust already bothered people like the philosopher Plato, one of the earliest and greatest writers in Western civilization (Burger 1980; Gee 2007a; Rowe 1986). Plato thought that writing would lead to the destruction of people's memory capacity. They would no longer remember what they could store in written texts. When asked to defend their views, people would not consult their own minds and memories, but, rather, point to a text.

Plato was concerned that people would claim to know what they really did not know (through personal insight, in their "souls") but had only read. They would not investigate questions for themselves, come to their own conclusions about what was right, and be able to defend these conclusions. Skipping this effort, they would rely on written texts and, ultimately, the experts or institutions who told them to trust these texts.

Plato was also bothered that a written text cannot be interrogated like a person can. If I disagree with people I can challenge them and they can respond. We can engage in a dialogue. But if I challenge a written text it will say nothing in response. There is no dialogue. Written texts are mute and, ultimately, experts and institutions speak for them and through them.

Finally, Plato was troubled by how texts can be distanced from their authors (who, he believed, were the ultimate authorities on what their texts meant). Texts can be interpreted by readers in ways an author would disavow.

Plato's concerns were well founded, of course. People's memories are not nearly as good as they were before writing, or in the Middle Ages when oral culture was still strong and few people could read or write. People do often claim to know something just because they have read it and not because they have reflected on and investigated the topic thoroughly. And, of course, books do not talk back when we challenge them and their authors are rarely available to speak for their books. As we have said, literacy is a technology, and there are always losses and gains with a new technology.

What makes a text trustworthy also comes into question when the whole notion of expertise is in crisis, as it is. We thought we could trust texts written by an expert like Alan Greenspan or, at least, the texts that comprise his discipline of economics. Given the current global economic crisis and Greenspan's admission that he did not anticipate it, why should we trust such texts or the experts and institutions that warrant them?

Literacy gave rise to a proliferation of different types of language and different types of texts. In turn, this proliferation gave rise to a proliferation of experts and a proliferation of institutions to support these experts. All this was to establish trust, a trust in crisis today. A related effect of all these proliferations was the erosion of the value of what we can call the "lifeworld" (Habermas 1984). The lifeworld is the "world" of "everyday people," the world that people who are not specialists or experts (or who are not at the time speaking as specialists or experts) can claim to know.

In an oral culture, there are many things that are considered within the realm of everyday people's knowledge. In these realms, people trust "common sense" or "what everyone knows." With the rise of literacy that area became progressively smaller. In more and more domains, experts claim that what everyday people know is not really true or trustworthy.

Whether air is really polluted or not, and how much pollution is dangerous, is settled by experts, not everyone who is breathing the air. The same is true of our water and food. Experts decide how children should be raised and what constitutes "abuse" (e.g. spanking), not parents. Whether hip-hop or video games are "art" is not decided by everyday consumers, but by expert designers and critics.

But experts often disagree. Dueling experts dispute global warming and the health hazards of carbon dioxide in the air. Here, again, the issue of trust arises. Are the experts disagreeing because they really do not know the truth or, at least, really disagree about the facts? Or are they disagreeing because some of them have been paid by big corporations to promote a particular viewpoint, or to receive publicity?

We know that cigarette companies and their paid experts lied about the health effects of smoking for decades because they did not want to lose money. Drug companies underwrite experts to make claims that advantage the drug companies and not necessarily consumers. Coal companies sponsor studies on global warming that support the interests of coal companies and coal mining, but which may or may not be trustworthy in regard to global warming.

The trust problem goes much deeper than mere lying. If and when we trust experts who claim that the earth is warming, with very bad potential consequences, we are still faced with experts in other fields who have competing views about the nature of these consequences and how to respond. Economists and politicians tell us that the economic impacts are more important than the environmental ones. Technological experts tell us that they will come up with a technical "fix" and that we need not worry too much about the dire warnings of the environmentalists. The coal and oil companies tell us that even if the world is warming due to our reliance on their products, other pollutants have greater effects (e.g. cow "emissions" are worse than car emissions) and, in any case, they will make "cleaner" oil and coal. Other experts tell us there is no such thing as "clean coal."

No one needs to lie for us to be confused and not know whom to trust. Plato would claim that we long ago gave up the responsibility to check the facts and develop our own understandings. Once we gave this responsibility to written texts, experts, and institutions, with their competing interests and claims, our current confusion was inevitable.

Our point here is *not* that there are no facts. It is not that there is no knowledge we can trust. One reason we rely on experts is that it is hard and time consuming for any one person to acquire all the knowledge they need to make good decisions. But we will see in Chapter 11 that today, with digital media, experts and everyday people can pool their knowledge and render technical matters much more readily accessible.

Our point is that while literacy gave rise to knowledge-producing experts and institutions, it also gave rise to a massive trust issue that has gotten worse with time and is at a crisis point today. This crisis is not caused primarily by religious beliefs that conflict with scientific theories and evidence (about, for example, evolution or the age of the earth), but by the proliferation of complexity, complex systems, and risk in a global world. To compound the problem, these systems are intertwined. The human and the natural interact today as they never have before. Weather, once considered an act of God, is now partly caused by human actions, as global warming helps cause storms and the heat island effect in cities makes them hotter at night as all the concrete releases the heat it has stored throughout the day.

Trust: Empirical evidence and ideology

In human history, people have had two basic ways to answer the question of why what they have said or written should be trusted. One way is to offer evidence and the other is to rest one's claims on authority. We want to be clear what these two ways to recruit trust really mean, since they are still utilized but have been greatly transformed by literacy.

One way is "empirical evidence." In an oral culture, or in everyday life today, when speakers offer empirical evidence for their claims this means three things: first, they are basing what they have said on observations they have made; second, they believe that others could observe, and, perhaps, already have observed, the same things; third, if they or some other trustworthy person makes observations that contradict their claims, this either lowers the speakers' confidence in their claims, makes them give up these claims, or at least makes them recheck their observations.

When people make empirical claims—for example, that the earth is billions of years old—they do not expect their status, power, or authority to win over an audience apart from empirical evidence, though status, power, and authority might play a role in deciding between two competing claims that both are supported by evidence of some decent sort.

The other way to gain trust is authority. In an oral culture, and even in our current everyday life, when speakers use authority to support their claims, this means the following: they are basing their claims on a belief system that is sanctioned by some "higher authority" rather than empirical observations. This authority can be many different things. It can be God, gods, ancestors, elders, a claim to noble birth, a claim to great intelligence or insight, or stories or myths passed down across the generations.

People believe the earth is less than 10,000 years old on the basis of the authority of the Bible and their church leaders. For many centuries in the West, people believed claims about the world or about the human body because the "ancients" (Aristotle and Galen) made them, not because of evidence (in fact, many of them were not correct) (Brown 1988; Laqueur 1990). In totalitarian countries, some things are held to be true just because the dictator says they are.

There are, and probably always have been, disputes about the boundaries between empirical evidence and authority. We are not concerned with those boundaries right now. Rather, we are concerned with two very old ways to answer the trust question. These are two different "games" with truth and trust, if we can put the matter that way.

Empirical evidence and authority are two different ways to satisfy the trust question. With the advent of literacy, these ways of establishing "truth" changed in dramatic ways, moving from local practices to large-scale "universal" enterprises. They eventually became science and "religions of the book." Let's look at each in turn.

Religion

In oral cultures, religion is local. It is a system of beliefs that evolve within a given group. These beliefs speak to fundamental questions the group has, based on their own unique history and environment. Often the beliefs are connected to the group's ancestors, explaining where they originated, providing a basis for shared practices such as coming-of-age ceremonies, or interpreting natural phenomena such as floods or drought.

So, for example, some Aboriginal groups that lived in the desert in Australia have a mythology about "The Dreaming," a sacred time in which ancestral spirit beings created the world (Isaacs 2006). There are dreamtime stories about the creation of sacred places, people, animals and plants, as well as laws and customs. Some of the stories involve dreamtime creatures (e.g. the dreamtime snake) traveling across the land and creating its geological features. Even today Aboriginals can use these stories, often in the form of songs, to find their way through the desert. Modern researchers have found that some geological features mentioned in the songs, features which no longer exist, did exist in the long past and the songs are accurate.

Dreamtime stories contain values and beliefs by which Aboriginals even today live their lives. They are constitutive of their spirituality and world view. But they are local, tied tightly to the landscape in which the Aboriginals have lived and the practices they used in order to survive in that landscape (for example, to quickly get to a faraway area where one saw rain falling, groups would use dreamtime songs to cross the desert; sometimes another group knew the continuation of the song when the original group came to the end of their territory and the end of the song as they knew it). Obviously, Aboriginal spiritual beliefs are local enough that they would make little sense as a religion for everyone in the world, regardless of where and how they lived.

Some questions are universal to human existence, questions like how did we get here, what does it all mean, and what happens after death. Even these universal questions had distinctive and local answers within each culture. For example, different cultures often had their own story of creation that explained how they came to be and why they were special as a people.

Writing gave rise to what are called the "religions of the book," including Christianity, Islam, and Judaism. With literacy, the religious beliefs, for example, of multiple and related Semitic peoples living in Middle Eastern deserts could be written down (as the Bible) and spread across the world. Jesus Christ's ideas about religious reforms in local versions of the Jewish religion could spread as the basis for a "universal church." The same kind of dissemination was possible for Islam when the Koran was written down.

The Roman emperor Constantine's conversion to Christianity in AD 312 allowed state power to meld with religious power and to enforce religious orthodoxy. The melding of state power and religious power has, of course, occurred in both Islam and Judaism in various ways at various times and places in history.

Religions of the book claim to speak to universal questions and issues, not local ones. Their beliefs and values spread across widely diverse geographical and cultural groups. Yet these beliefs and values were originally developed to make sense to a culturally and geographically specific group of people (e.g. Semitic desert dwellers in the case of the Old Testament). What was once local has become global. Such texts must now be interpreted as relevant to cultures and places far away in space and time from their origin.

Imagine that the religious beliefs of the early Germanic peoples who lived in forests and organized their cultural groups quite differently than did Semitic desert dwellers had been written down and spread across the world (which they were not). The world would have had a quite different problem of translation, of how to make such beliefs "universal."

It is not surprising that a massive problem of interpretation arises for religions of the book. Today, in the United States, those who preach a "prosperity gospel" claim that Christ wanted people to be rich. Others emphasize his feelings for the poor and his demands that people give up their riches. There are many disputes in Islam about how to interpret the Koran and related writings, as well as how (or how not) to make them relevant to the modern world. It is not surprising, then, that there have been centuries of controversies over how to interpret these religions' books. People have fought over these interpretations both peacefully and violently.

When religions become universal, thanks to books that can travel far and wide, fights over which religion is "right" can become far more widespread than in any oral culture. These fights over religious beliefs can have very high stakes. Given that people want badly to believe that their god is really the God, fights over religion can become fights over who is and who is not really human or worthy of respect.

Literacy gave rise to religions as major, international, "universal," and contesting enterprises. Religions often melded with state power for enforcement purposes. As we have seen so often with literacy, religious texts gave rise to experts and institutions to support these experts and enforce their authority. Experts ("priests") tell the "laity" the "proper" interpretation of scripture ("God's word") and institutions (e.g. religious courts, the church) arise to enforce their authority.

Science

Literacy helped give rise to science. Science is today a "universal" international enterprise on the scale of religions of the book (Latour 1987, 1999; Star 1989). It is the outgrowth, thanks to literacy, of the "empirical evidence" response to the trust question.

There is an irony in the historical growth of science. For centuries after the discovery of writing and even print, people who engaged in early scientific investigations (for example, the study of human anatomy) very often used an authority-based approach to the trust question. They claimed that what they said was true and trustworthy because old authorities like Aristotle and Galen had said it, though they too usually had little empirical support for their claims.

For example, people in the West believed for hundreds of years that male and female bodies were identical, save that males' genitals popped out and females' did not, because males were "hotter" than women with a heat that was thought to be both physical and spiritual and which made their genital organs expand (Laqueur 1990). They also believed that both men and women ejaculated sperm when they engaged in intercourse. They believed these things because Galen (an early, great, and revered Greek doctor) said they were true centuries earlier.

When Rome converted to Christianity, the Church became a source of authority in competition with the ancients like Aristotle and Galen. For example,

St Thomas Aquinas interpreted Aristotle in ways that made his ideas acceptable to the Church. Galileo discovered that even scientists were meant to take the Church's word on matters about the stars and planets in the sky (despite what he saw through his telescope).

Eventually, and this is one of the great triumphs of the Renaissance and the later Enlightenment periods in the West, empirical evidence came into its own. Authority, whether of Aristotle or the Church, was no longer, in science, an acceptable answer to the trust question. Empirical evidence was the only acceptable answer (Shapin & Schaffer 1985; Star 1989).

However, a problem arose with empirical evidence. Ironically, the problem was not all that different to the problem that arose with the books of the religions: a problem with interpretation. As science developed around scientists' observations of the world, it gradually became apparent that different observers often saw different things or interpreted what they saw in different ways (Latour 1987, 1999; Myers 1990; Pickering 1995; Shapin & Schaffer 1985; Star 1989). For example, in the early days of studying nature scientifically, scientists brought back different reports on what certain animals did or had different interpretations of what they had seen. Even with early laboratory experiments, for example, to settle whether nature ever gave rise to a vacuum or whether some life forms spontaneously generated from decaying material, different people who observed the experiments saw different things or explained what they saw in different ways (Shapin & Schaffer 1985).

Science eventually developed a whole apparatus of methods, techniques, and theories to control and tame observation (Latour 1999; Myers 1990). The controlled scientific experiment, often done in a laboratory, was one such device. This, of course, led directly (as we now fully expect) to a proliferation of experts and institutions.

In the past, a British parson could go out and observe beetles. He could then write his observations as an empirical contribution to science. He might claim to be a more seasoned and experienced observer than others, but, in principle, they could see what he had seen. But today, any observation and observer must be vetted by experiments, scientific tools, methods, techniques, and theories all supported by experts (professionals—the parson was an amateur) and institutions. No longer could an everyday person, or even a seasoned observer like the parson, claim knowledge based just on observation. The empirical evidence answer to the trust question had changed. It became a large-scale, technical, non-local enterprise supported by experts and their institutions, as did religion.

We are not claiming that science is "ideological" and that there is really no deep difference between the empirical evidence answer to the trust question and the authority one. When medicine was based on Aristotle's and Galen's authority, many more people died than they do with modern empirical medicine. Nor are we claiming that for all purposes empirical evidence is better than authority. There are, indeed, questions not open to empirical evidence. What we are concerned with, though, is the crisis of experts and institutions, a crisis which, we will see, affects both science and religion.

What science and religion share in the modern world is this: science took away a good deal of meaning and authority from everyday people's observations of the secular world. The secular world became the preserve of experts whom everyday people had to trust. Religions of the book (what we could call "big religion" in analogy to "big science") took away a good deal of the meaning and authority of people's locally, culturally, historically, and contextually based sense of the spiritual world. The spiritual world became the preserve of experts whom everyday people had to trust.

Humans have always contested and fought this erosion of their powers of knowing. Historically it often has been a losing battle in face of the massive scale of science and religion, and the ways both are often supported by the powers of the state in the modern world. But the tide of battle, perhaps, is changing. As we have seen, experts and institutions, and their claims for trust, are in crisis. Digital media, as we will see later, are both contributing to this crisis and offering some ways out of it.

7

SCHOOL

Writing, print, and reading

This chapter is about literacy at school, though we will start with a discussion of the transition from handwritten books to printed books and how that changed the nature of reading. Literacy, as we have said, is a delivery system for oral language. However, in school it has long taken on a life of its own quite separate from oral language. We expect schools to "teach literacy" but, by and large, do not expect them to teach oral language.

Every child in school already knows some version of an oral language. Nonetheless, there are many varieties of oral language that children do not know. These include the varieties of oral language associated with academic books and content. These varieties of language are sometimes called "academic language" (Gee 2004; Schleppegrell 2004) or "academic languages," since there are different varieties of academic language associated with different academic domains like mathematics, physics, and the social sciences. There are also specialized varieties of oral language used in the public sphere. These are varieties of language like those used in courts, public forums, business places, workplaces, and in formal interactions like job interviews. Children do not come to school knowing these types of language either.

Before moving on, let us say something about types of literacy in the sense of different types of writing. In transportation, the transitions from horses to cars to planes were profoundly consequential. Each transition gave rise to major changes in human societies, cultures, and the global world. So, too, with the transition from handwriting to print.

In cultures like ancient Rome and the Western Middle Ages that had no print and copied their books by handwriting, books were expensive, rare, and slow to produce (Goody 1986; Olson 1996; Saenger 1997). Few people owned books, few could read, and even fewer could write. When people read books, they read them over and over again. They read them slowly and reflected on what the books said. They expected books to be about deep and important matters, worthy of slow, meditative, and repeated reading. Books were too hard to produce and expensive to own to be about trivial matters. Thus, early books in the West tended to be about religion and philosophy.

Handwritten books in the West, in Rome, for instance, were often written with no spaces between the words and with the letters all the same size (Saenger 1997). This made reading difficult. It also caused people to read out loud (or at least mumble) as they said the strings of letters out loud and juggled them in their minds to find the word boundaries (e.g. try reading thefewthingsthatgobumpinthenight).

People did not expect or want reading to be easy or widespread. With few books to read and a lifetime to read them, the few people who could read had plenty of time to learn and practice (over and over again on the same books). Since books were devoted to profound topics, they were not for everyone, but reserved for people who were (thought to be) thoughtful, educated, elite, and intelligent people.

An important transition before print was adding spaces between words and using letters of different sizes that were easier to distinguish. This made reading easier and potentially available to more people. This transition was caused, in part, by the collapse of the Roman Empire and the arrival of the Dark Ages. Monks in Europe copied ancient Greek and Roman manuscripts in order to preserve them, but no longer understood Latin and Greek as native languages (Cahill 1996; Saenger 1997). They wanted to make the texts more accessible, both to ensure their continued existence and for readers who were not native speakers of Greek or Latin.

In the days of handwritten books in the West no book was written in a local or "vulgar" language (i.e. languages other than Greek and Latin). When the monks copied the books of Greece and Rome, including the copies of these books originally preserved in the Islamic countries of the Middle East, they sometimes wrote notes (and even limericks) in their local languages (like Gaelic in Ireland, English in England, and so forth) in the margins of the manuscripts (copies) they were producing (Saenger 1997). The margins did not "count." This "marginal" practice gave rise to a revolution, the eventual production of books and knowledge in languages other than Greek and Latin, and eventually the death of Latin as the language of religion and scholarship.

In the history of literacy, change regularly comes from the margins. Practices we see as aberrant and marginal often represent the future. We will see that this is happening today in and around school.

Print, invented around 1450, was one of the great inventions and transitions in human history. It eventually made books and reading widely accessible, breaking the hold elites had on reading. Print gave rise to wide readership and book ownership. It also gave rise (just as the old elites with their rare handwritten books would have predicted) to books on any and all topics, trivial and not. People read more and faster (and silently), but reread and reflected and meditated on what they read less than they had before. Many people have bemoaned that digital media have killed reflective, slow, meditative reading of "deep" texts. But print plunged in the sword first and best.

Print did not make these changes quickly or easily. Elites fought back. Arguments raged in many countries for centuries (well into the nineteenth) about whether poor people and working-class people (or women or minorities) should be able to read (Gee 2007a). What would ensure they read correctly and would not question established beliefs?

Sweden was the first country in the West to mandate universal reading ability (in the sixteenth century) and to achieve it by the 1800s (Gee 2007a; Graff *et al.* 2009; Johansson 1977). They accomplished this by making parents, in particular, mothers, responsible for teaching their families to read the Bible. In turn, mothers were supervised by regular visits from the minister. Reading had a religious purpose and was carefully monitored. In Sweden the Lutheran church and state were closely linked and, thus, the state could enforce a religious reading campaign.

After the Protestant Revolution in the West, Catholics and Protestants fought over whether the laity (everyday people) should read the Bible for themselves. Protestants argued they should, but then faced the problem (as in Sweden) of how to ensure "correct" reading. Catholics argued that they should not. Instead, the priest should tell the laity what the sacred texts meant. Either way, neither side was comfortable with people interpreting the Bible on their own if their interpretation threatened the authority of the church or the state (Protestant sects that tolerated diverse interpretations experienced, as a result, a proliferation of divisions within the original sect).

Print eventually but slowly made reading nearly universal among the population in many (but not all) countries. However, the ability to write has always been much less common and has never become universal, even in modern countries today. Many people in the United States, for instance, cannot write as well as they can read, do not write much, or cannot write at all. Even when writing became widespread in societies, it was much later than universal reading. Why?

Writing is the production of meaning, not just "consumption." Such production on the part of everyday people (non-elites) has always seemed even more dangerous to church and state than reading. In the case of reading, the state or a church can control what is produced and distributed (by producing it themselves or authorizing only some people to produce it). They can censor its content. But if everyday people, or dissidents, begin to write and distribute their own texts outside the supervision of state or church, there is less church and state control of what is written and distributed.

Of course, oral language is also hard to control and people can say things that "the powers that be" do not like. State and church in many societies have sought to restrict or control oral language. But oral language, until the age of audio recording and digital media, could not spread as widely as print.

Writing was deeply dangerous for state and church power because it was a form of production open, in principle, to everyone. Today this problem of open production is much more threatening for those in power. Thanks to digital media we live in an age where, at least potentially, anyone can produce almost anything (books, film, games, news, science, bombs, and so on).

Four factors in learning to read

1   Oral language

Early schooling in modern societies has become primarily about learning to read. Though some privileged children come to school already knowing how to read, for most children the process of learning to read starts at home but finishes at school. For some poor children the whole process goes on at school.

It has long been felt that by teaching all children to read well, school could "level the playing field" for success in school. This is, however, not true. Even when poor children learn to read well in school, they still often (though, of course, not always) over time fare less well than more privileged children, especially if they attend schools with many other poor children (Chall *et al.* 1990; Gee 2004; Juel 1988; Juel *et al.* 1986).

Learning to read involves four interrelated factors. Unfortunately these factors are not as closely connected in school as they should be. First, a learner must know an oral language (Dickinson & Neuman 2006; Dickinson *et al.* 2010; Gee 2004). This is, of course, true of most learners.

There are also learners who know one oral language but must learn to read in a second language that they do not know or do not know very well (for example, Spanish-speaking immigrant children in the United States). A learner can learn to read a second language without oral skills in that language (using, in part, translation skills). But again, this is difficult. It is easier to learn to read in one's first language and then to transfer this skill to a second language that one has already learned, or is learning, orally as well.

For all learners, oral language is an important foundation for learning to read and write. A child's success in school, from second grade on to high school and beyond, correlates highly with their oral vocabularies at the age of five (Gee 2004; Sénéchal *et al.* 2006). The importance of this vocabulary is not a matter of understanding everyday words (like "candy," "Mom," and "cat"). It is a matter of understanding more "book-related" and "formal" words (words like "encourage," "allow," "argument," and "dinosaur"). The child's vocabulary is a marker of how much adult language and language connected to books the child has heard. This factor is a strong predictor of school success.

Another indicator of the importance of oral language is that a learner's ability to comprehend written language is highly correlated with their ability to comprehend oral language (Biemiller 2003). The human brain uses the same structures to comprehend oral language and written language (Kintsch 1998). It has no special-purpose structures devoted to comprehending just written language. Furthermore, a learner's oral comprehension skills set the limit, at least in the early stages of learning to read, of their reading comprehension (Biemiller 2003).

2   Written language

The second factor in learning to read is learning how written language delivers oral language. Any writing system is based on a set of conventions that must be mastered. In English, we use an alphabet (26 letters that represent 44 phonemes or speech sounds) and various conventions about how to write words and sentences and punctuate them. We also have certain conventions about how to structure different genres or types of writing (e.g. narratives, essays, reports, exposition, description, and so forth).

The conventions of writing are profoundly different from the conventions that govern how we speak. Writing conventions were intentionally designed by humans in the relatively recent past. Some writing systems are easier than others (e.g. it is easier to spell in Spanish than it is in English and learning to read and write in Mandarin, without an alphabet, is much harder than learning in either Spanish or English).

Learning literacy does not require overt direct teaching, though that is one way to learn it. But it does require interventions beyond talking to children (Pinker 1994), though talking to children does turn out to be very important for learning to read (Hart & Risely 1995). Adults must design children's environments overtly and intentionally, in some respects, to allow them to learn literacy (Adams 1990; Crowley & Jacobs 2002; Gee 2004; Neuman 2010; Neuman & Celano 2006). Adults have to supply texts and it helps massively if they engage in a whole variety of literacy practices in the home: practices like book reading; asking questions of the child while reading to him or her; talking about books; relating books to other books and media and the world; encouraging children to do pretend readings; allowing the child to see adults reading and writing and talking about reading and writing; and talking to children using a wide vocabulary about one's experiences and the world beyond things that are just here and now.

All these designed interactions around books can be called a form of teaching. In this sense (and not in the limited sense of skill and drill and overt teaching alone), literacy requires teaching and oral language does not. Learning literacy is very sensitive to home-based factors (such as how many books are in the home and how caregivers interact with children around books) before and after the child has gone to school. But, we would argue, this is not just true of learning literacy, but of many sorts of learning, most especially learning associated with school (e.g. learning science).

3   Comprehension of social languages

The third factor in learning to read is learning what (and how) written language means (this is usually talked about in terms of "comprehension"). This, at first sight, should not be a problem. Written language means just what the oral language it delivers means, so long as one can decode the written language. But comprehension is not this simple.

We mentioned above that the human brain uses the same capacities to compre-hend oral and written language. However, here we come to a crucial point that is rarely given much overt attention in school: there are many different varieties of oral language (Gee 2004, 2007a, 2010).

Every human being, barring severe disabilities, learns a vernacular version of their native language early in life. This is the form of language we use as everyday people speaking as everyday people and not as experts or specialists. English speakers, like the speakers of all languages, speak their vernacular style or variety somewhat differently based on their home and community cultures and dialects. But they all speak one such variety and all varieties are, from a linguistic point of view, equal, equally good, and rooted in long histories of human communication.

There are other forms of oral language, non-vernacular forms, which people learn later in life. They learn to speak like carpenters, biologists, lawyers, street gang members, video game fanatics, accountants, and many other identities. These non-vernacular varieties are not mastered early in life and not everyone knows them. Furthermore, no one knows them all.

Different varieties of a language that are based on what their speakers are trying to be (a carpenter or a lawyer) or do (carpentry or law) are sometimes called "regis-ters" (Gee 2010). We call them "social languages" (different varieties of a language that vary not only by where people live or were born—this is what dialects are—but also in terms of what they are and do). The vernacular is one social language all humans have (again, barring very severe disorders). There are many others, connected to roles and activities ("occupations") that humans have invented.

Here is an example of what we mean. All native speakers can construct a sentence like "Hornworms sure vary a lot in how well they grow" (as long as they know what hornworms are) in their oral vernacular social languages, though speakers may differ a bit in exactly how they say it. A sentence like "Hornworm growth exhibits a significant amount of statistical variation" is not a sentence every native speaker can spontaneously say or write. It is not in the vernacular. Rather, it is a specialist social language of an academic sort, connected to biology. A person who does not know this social language, if they can decode print, can pronounce it. But their oral vernacular comprehension skills will not help them to understand it fully. They need additional comprehension skills, rooted in the ability to speak or at least think in this variety of language.

Vernacular language is the basic form of human language. There are next to no (probably no) grammatical structures in a non-vernacular social language that are not present in the vernacular. For example, any vernacular can produce a structure like "hornworm growth" (a nominalization, or noun made from a verb), as in, for example, "my love (for you)" or "John's gift (to you)." The vernacular is the resource for all non-vernacular varieties. But these varieties use this resource in distinctive ways. For example, many academic social languages use complex nominalizations as subjects ("hornworm growth"), coupled with abstract verbs (like "exhibit") and complex phrases with modifiers ("a significant amount of statistical variation").

Written versions of a given social language (e.g. the language of lawyers or anime film critics) are tied to oral versions of the same social language. When we speak a given specialist social language, like the language of biology, we often (but not always) speak it in a somewhat less formal way than we write it. People can most certainly learn to read social languages (like the language of biology) that they cannot speak fully. But, in the end, this is often a problem if they want to work within the community who uses this social language.

So the third factor in learning to read is learning how to make meaning and comprehend in varieties of language beyond our vernacular. Knowing just how to read and write in one's vernacular is, in today's world, a very limited skill indeed.

There is a long-known phenomenon in school called the "fourth-grade slump," when children seem to be learning to read in the early grades, and even pass reading tests, but do not seem to read well by around fourth grade (American Federation of Teachers 2003; Chall & Jacobs 2003; Gee 2008b). This phenomenon is caused by teaching early reading only as the ability to read vernacular language and not as the ability to read content that is expressed in non-vernacular language (Gee 2004, 2008b). By fourth grade (often earlier today), children confront the first and earliest versions of complex academic non-vernacular language as they learn social studies, math, and science. Suddenly they have difficulty reading, because they cannot comprehend such varieties of language, and often not because they cannot decode print and comprehend vernacular language.

Many homes with highly educated parents start their children's preparation for the sorts of academic language they will see in school quite early. For example, such parents often encourage their young children to develop what have been called "islands of expertise" (Crowley & Jacobs 2002). These are interests that lead the child to become a "little expert" on interests such as dinosaurs, trains, castles, horses. The topic does not really matter. What matters is that the parents buy the child books and other products related to the interest, take the child on trips to see relevant exhibits and museums, and otherwise help to extend the child's knowledge in this area. More importantly, the parents talk to the child, when discussing the child's island of expertise, in more adult and school-like language.

One mother talking to her 3-year-old "little expert" on dinosaurs said things like (Crowley & Jacobs 2002: 343, 345):

> That's what it [the card] says, see look egg, egg … Replica of a dinosaur egg. From the oviraptor.
> And that's from the Cretaceous period. And that was a really, really long time ago.
> And this is … the hind claw. What's a hind claw? [pause] A claw from the back leg from a velociraptor. And you know what …
> They use their claws to cut open their prey, right?

Educators call words like "replica," "prey," "period," and "hind" Tier 2 words (Beck *et al.* 2002). Tier 1 words are everyday vernacular words like "cat," "go," "home," and "ball." Tier 3 are technical terms in specific areas, words like "allele," "quark," "hydron," and "electron." Tier 2 words are more formal words that occur across many academic, specialist, and public-sphere domains and in a wide variety of written texts, words like "process," "state," "account," "probable," "occurrence," "maintain," "benevolent," and so forth. Such words are foundational for success in school, certainly from the fourth grade on, and some families ensure that their children get an early start on learning such words, orally and in print.

Different social languages involve more than words ("vocabulary"). They involve different grammatical conventions as well (Gee 2010). We saw this in the example sentences about hornworms above. But words are an early foundation on which to build future social language learning, words used in talk, not memorized on lists. At the same time, parents like the mother above use more complex syntax (sentence structures) as they talk to their children in areas where their children have special or more expert knowledge.

4 Social practices

The fourth factor in learning to read is learning what people *do* with written language (and one thing they do is speak it). It is not sufficient to know how a sentence like "Hornworm growth exhibits a significant amount of statistical variation" is spoken (an aspect of our first factor). It is not enough to know how it is written or decoded into sound (an aspect of our second factor). It is not enough to know what it means (an aspect of our third factor). None of this makes sense without understanding *why* anyone would say, write, or interpret such a sentence, or have any desire to do so. Understanding why this matters depends on knowing what can be *done* by saying such a thing, that is, what functions it can have (Gee 2004, 2007a, 2010).

Here we need to go beyond learning "literacy" and "written language" and see them as part and parcel of a larger process of learning social languages. Learning in school involves learning written language associated with academic content. Such content is connected to specific social languages (e.g. the language of science, civics, mathematics, literature, literary criticism, art, and so forth). These social languages are heavily associated with writing, but they are also spoken. Literacy learning in school is really about learning social languages (Gee 2004).

Just as cars were invented for a purpose, so too were different specialist social languages, from the language of accountants to that of *Yu-Gi-Oh!* cards. People would not be very motivated to learn to drive if they had no idea why anyone drove, had no idea what they could do or where they could get by driving, or no desire to get anywhere. So, too, with specialist social languages. Very often the only reason a child in school wants to learn or use academic varieties of language is to get a good grade.

Now we face a main problem with school as we know it. People learn to drive because they want to drive cars. But people often cannot, or do not want to, use a specialist form of language (written or oral) for the purposes for which it is intended. It's a car they don't see the need for, don't want, and may even fear. They cannot or do not want to go there.

A sentence like "Hornworm growth exhibits a significant amount of statistical variation" has a number of functions among the people who speak and write this way (e.g. biologists). One of these functions is to state claims based on statistics and other quantitative tools that control, tame, and "trump" observation. It may look to everyday people, and to children raising hornworms in school, like "hornworms vary a lot in how well they grow." But the biologist can say such observations are not trustworthy. Large visual differences in hornworm growth can be statistically insignificant and small ones can be statistically significant. We—and the child— cannot really know by observing and interacting with hornworms. We need to be familiar with and have allegiance to tools (language tools, statistical tools, and other tools) that biologists invented, use, and "own" for describing hornworm growth (and other biological phenomena).

In order really to understand "Hornworm growth exhibits a significant amount of statistical variation," one needs to know why one would want to "tame" observation in this way. One also must want to do so. A child, of course, may have no such knowledge or interest. Worse, the child may much prefer his or her own observations of and interactions with hornworms (cute green worms with yellow horns) to tools, tests, and techniques owned by experts and institutions to which he or she does not and may never feel any allegiance. At the very least, someone or something must give the child a "job" (function) he or she understands how to accomplish and desires to accomplish using the sentence and language in it.

Written language and non-vernacular specialist social languages (oral or written) are used for different functions within distinctive practices. Here the term "practice" just means something a distinctive group of people does. Carrying out an experiment in a lab is a practice. Trading *Yu-Gi-Oh!* cards in a schoolyard is a practice. Writing a report on the local population for the city council is a practice. Using geometry to design and build something in *Second Life* is a practice. Doing geometry problems to get a good grade is a practice, too.

Each practice makes use of a social language to help accomplish a particular function or job. Thus, "Hornworm growth exhibits a significant amount of statistical variation" can be used to do a specific job in a domain like biology (e.g. argue over distributions and their significance beyond the results of mere observations).

The bottom line is that the learner must learn the practices (both understand them and want to do them) that distinctive non-vernacular specialist social languages (of the sort connected to school content) were designed to support (or innovative but related uses of such language). School usually introduces practices last (after the so-called "basic skills"), never really incorporates them, uses confused versions of them, or is never really clear to children about how what they are learning is tied to actual practices or who uses them (and cares about them) in the world. Small wonder, then, that literacy learning can be so hard in school.

Reading in school

Learning to read, write, and speak specialist social languages associated with school content (or learning social languages anywhere) is like learning a sport and joining a team. Lectures, skill and drill, and practice by yourself take you only so far in trying to learn to play basketball. A large part of such learning requires playing with others on a team (formal or pick up). It is the team sport and how the game is played that give its moves, skills, and facts meaning, purpose, and motivates people to learn them. So, too, with any social language.

One core problem with school is that the social languages around which school literacy is based are tied to "teams" that students are not part of and do not get to join (e.g. scientists in science labs). Further, the "sports" these teams play, such as physics, biology, literary criticism, social science, or geometry, are not necessarily ones learners want to play. Worse yet, they are no longer the type of sports most productive academics and researchers play.

Today, most academic research is not organized around old disciplinary and department labels like chemistry, biology, or sociology. Researchers from different disciplines work collaboratively on shared "themes" or "challenges" that require multiple methods and the invention of new shared methods and language (Collins & Evans 2007; Olson *et al.* 2008; Shrum *et al.* 2007; Wagner 2008). Work on global warming, human–nature interactions, environment degradation, the global economy, urban planning, global poverty, the rise and fall of civilizations, space travel, new sources of energy, and complex adaptive systems of many different sorts are what now define how people work, not just a disciplinary label.

Further, disciplinary labels like "biology" and "anthropology" do not name any unitary perspective or research methodology, and hide a wealth of conflict and disagreement. Cultural anthropologists, archeologists, and physical anthropologists may all be in an anthropology department, but they are aligned with different disciplines and do not always get along or see themselves as alike or even compatible. So, too, with ecologists, microbiologists, geneticists, and molecular biologists in biology departments. And, to put it mildly, the literary criticism, cultural studies, applied linguistics, composition-rhetoric, and creative writing teachers and researchers in English departments are a diverse lot with plenty of different sorts of contacts outside their department. Productive modern academics often play on a different team (organized around an interdisciplinary collaborative theme or challenge) than the one that pays them (their university department).

Schools organize their teaching and tests around "content" that originated from and is loosely connected to academic disciplines. These disciplines are now often little more than budgetary units in universities and labels for nearly meaningless majors in college (like "Anthropology"). Learners in school get content that is really made up of skills, facts, and "moves" connected to a game played by teams they will rarely or never join, teams now playing different games in any case.

Schools seek to "solve" this problem in one of several ways. The most common solution is to teach young people the content, skills, and "moves" connected (albeit very loosely) to academic disciplines without letting them use the content, skills, and "moves" in a real game as part of real team (participating as a member of a group doing actual scientific research, for example). We have known for decades that this approach to school leads, as one would predict, to enabling students to pass multiple-choice, fact-based tests (at best), but not to their ability to use facts, skills, or tools to actually solve problems in the world (Gee 2004).

A second popular solution, sometimes associated with more liberal or progressive approaches to education, is to allow children to engage in activities where they "pretend to be scientists," for example. They engage in science-like activities (e.g. studying pollution in a local pond). Sometimes these activities are unrecognizable in comparison to authentic scientific activities as they are actually carried out and accepted in professional practice. Sometimes, the specialist social languages of science are actually ignored, dropped, or misused. In some instances, the activities are more authentic, more like playing the "real" game.

This "pretend" approach can be done well and powerfully (though it usually is not). It still has the problem that kids are playing versions of a game that they will often not really ever play in anything like the way it is played in the world outside of school. Educators often try to explain this problem away by saying that children are learning to be "good citizens"; for example, they will be able to understand complex scientific issues as they impinge on public policy. Whether this is a worthy goal for schools or not—it probably is—schools are, at least currently, a failure at attaining this goal. Most Americans actually know little about science and our students fare poorly in international comparisons on science (e.g. on issues like knowing what sorts of questions are open to scientific investigation and which are not).

Today, for all the reasons we have discussed, school is in crisis. Much school knowledge does not lead to the ability to solve problems or innovate. But the current crisis goes further, and for this reason: today the problems of school are being solved out of school. The danger is that school will eventually be a relic institution if it does not, for the first time in a hundred years, really change and change radically. The need for school reform in the face of competition from out-of-school learning systems is the topic of the next chapter.

8

SCHOOL AND PASSIONATE AFFINITY SPACES

Essayist literacy in school

For a long time now, in a sense, school has "owned" literacy. School honors and rewards a narrow range of literacy practices. It also honors a narrow range of oral language practices connected to literacy. Further, it honors and rewards some literacy practices that are never or rarely used in life outside of school. Let's look at some of the major "ways with words" (Heath 1983) honored in school.

Ron and Suzanne Scollon (1981) have argued that the fundamental orientation to literacy in school is what they called "essayist literacy." Essayist literacy is a style of discourse that demands (written and spoken) formal and explicit language. An essay is focused on a single well-developed topic. Essays are written in the voice of the rational intellect for other rational intellects. As we discussed earlier, author and readers are, in that sense, "fictionalized." They are not writing and reading in terms of their own idiosyncratic and individual personalities (or they are seeking to hide them).

Historically, the nature of essayist literacy is a little more complicated than the above description implies (Bazerman 1988). Essays were a text form originally meant to present a personal point of view on a challenging or deep topic. This sounds like a pretty individualistic orientation. But, in fact, this personal point of view was supposed to be the point of view of an ultimately rational person who had special insight based on experience, education, elite birth, or expertise.

Think about how this view is reflected in expectations for an essay written for a college application today. Candidates have to present themselves as "special" (having a unique perspective to bring to the college), but not as idiosyncratic. Candidates typically share their beliefs and values, but cannot say they believe X because Uncle Fred told them. They have to claim something like their volunteer "service" (vacation) to the Caribbean led them to insights (that any rational person would share, if they, too, had had these experiences) about the toxic admixture of poverty and wealth in the developing world.

The word "essay" has come to stand for a wider range of argumentative forms. It now often includes such things as factual reports, biographical essays, editorials, and, sometimes, academic research papers. There is, of course, considerable value in well-argued and focused rational argumentation. But in school there are problems with the emphasis placed on essayist literacy as well. First, essays are often, out in the world, written by experts in the essay's topic. Students are typically just pretending to be experts, or at least being asked to pretend they are experts.

Second, essays in the world are usually written by people who care a good deal about their topic. Students often do not care about the topic, since typically they did not choose it. They are expected to pretend to care.

Third, in the everyday world, the essay as a way of intellectually confronting, at a fairly deep level, key human questions or dilemmas has pretty much been replaced, on the one hand, by (not always so rational) media and, on the other, by professional academic papers. The result is that students rarely encounter examples of essays in their daily lives, making this form seem even less relevant and giving students little exposure to models of good (or bad) essays.

Finally, the vast majority of people (including "powerful" and successful people like CEOs) do not write essays of any sort after they leave school. There is, of course, still a role for the essay in society, but its place in the ecology of literacy has changed considerably since its invention as a form in the sixteenth century.

School content

Another orientation to literacy in school is what we might call teaching "content literacy" (Gee 2004). In school, "content" is identified by labels like "algebra," "biology," "civics," and "literature." School content is loosely connected to academic disciplines. It is basically the "knowledge" (in a quite oversimplified form) such disciplines have produced over the years, sanctioned by authorities, commoditized into textbooks and similar texts. By the time such content gets to school, it becomes "what every educated person ought to know" (about science, for example, or history) or the "facts" and "information" every "informed" person ought to know.

There are many problems with content literacy. First, academic disciplines produce content with methods, tools, practices, and controversies that are essential to its production and necessary for evaluating that knowledge (as "content"). But schools present the content without the methods, practices, and controversies.

Second, as we said in the last chapter, cutting edge academics today often work collaboratively on themes or challenges that transcend a single discipline. Rather than teach "social studies" in school (a term for the "content" of the social sciences as this content is reduced to "facts" and information for school textbooks), perhaps schools should teach students urban planning where they could put the tools of various social sciences (economics, sociology, ecology, and political science) together to think about real problems and challenges. Perhaps they could even engage in this task collaboratively, each specializing in one area, teaching it to others, and all combining their knowledge and skills. There are digital tools today that allow young people to do just this in games that are like *SimCity*, but which are more realistic in regard to real urban planning (Shaffer 2007).

Third, a considerable amount of important knowledge today is produced outside of academic institutions, sometimes well outside them. It is produced in think tanks, businesses, workplaces, across the Internet, and, most distinctively today, in popular culture activities using digital media. We will describe an example of just this later in the chapter. Today students can engage in knowledge production outside of school, but often only engage in fact and information consumption in school.

Fourth, "content" (meaning information and facts) is today "cheap," that is, easy to get. It can be found all over the Internet. Understanding the methods for producing such content and reasons for trusting it (or not) is, however, not cheap or easy. School is still often about the former and not the latter.

Fifth, a tremendous amount of school "content"—"what every educated person should know"—is, in fact, not true or it is so oversimplified as to be misleading. Textbooks repeat what other textbooks have said, errors included (Gould 1985). To use an example of "content" from our field, linguistics, an oft-heard claim is that "Eskimo languages" have dozens or hundreds of words for snow. But this is not true (Pullum 1991).

Sixth, academic disciplines and newer cross-disciplinary research endeavors are not about producing "content," but about solving problems. The "content" (facts, information, skills) they produce is used as a set of tools to help them solve problems. School abstracts the content from the problems and we get students who can pass tests, but not solve problems. We mentioned in a previous chapter that students who can recite Newton's laws of motion often cannot apply those laws to solve a real world problem.

Seventh, much of the "content" any educated person will need to know in the future, out of school, has not yet been discovered. People need to be more adept at learning new things than storing old, oversimplified, sometimes false "facts." Increasingly school needs to prepare students for future learning (Bransford & Schwartz 1999).

Test literacy

A third orientation to literacy in school is what we can call "test literacy." Tests define what students should know and should be able to do. Today's tests often lead to knowledge and practices that are used nowhere else than in school. Take reading tests as an example. Such tests often (though this is now changing somewhat) involve reading short passages on many different topics (none of which the reader may care about) and answering questions about important or unimportant aspects of the passage (Hill & Larsen 2000). The questions are determined by test design (the need for scores to fall into a bell curve), not relevance to the passage or any real purpose connected to reading it.

On such short-passage tests, and even on tests now using longer, more connected passages, the questions are often ones that can be answered without reading the passages (Owen 1985). For example, we gave a fourth-grade "high-stakes" reading test with a long passage about monkeys to a first grader. We did not give him the passage, only the questions. He answered 80 percent of the questions correctly. He was from a privileged family and had read, heard, and seen a great deal about monkeys and other animals. His background knowledge was enough to answer the questions on a "reading" test meant for older children.

Such reading tests do indeed constitute a literacy practice, but it is a practice that is used nowhere else in life. In fact, there are aspects of this reading test practice that contradict what children are told elsewhere in school. On such tests (and, for example, on the SAT reading test), students are told not to make inferences about the text based on their experiences in the world (Owen 1985). This, by the way, is good advice for these tests; such tests punish test-takers for drawing on their own experiences rather than sticking to the information in the text alone. But elsewhere in school, students are told to use their experiences to understand and make connections to the texts. Of course, we typically draw on our experiences when reading outside of school.

Tests tell teachers and students what reading, science, mathematics, and other subjects are. Often, as with the reading tests we just discussed, they make these subjects something they never are or rarely are in life. It is an interesting fact that young people in countries that perform the best on international comparisons of science and math tend to have the least positive attitudes toward science and mathematics (TIMSS 2000a, 2000b). These tests, as all important tests, shape how people think about learning science and mathematics and the view of learning they give is, in fact, not terribly motivating or attractive to students, even when they can pass the tests.

Test literacy—learning to take tests and treating topics like reading and science the way tests suggest we should—has other interesting properties. One is that, in many cases, a standardized test that was designed in another state by a national company, taken on one day outside the course of normal instruction, trumps the assessment of the teacher who has been with the students for months. It trumps, as well, any assessment of how students have grown and developed across time, since a student who has made considerable progress and one who has not are judged the same if they get the same score. Yet Johnnie may have started way behind Janie and made much more progress in a given time period than she has.

We would only change our approach to testing if we wanted to change what and how schools teach. If we taught problem solving and the use of content (information, facts, and formulas) as tools for solving problems we would need new tests. In turn, we would get students who knew content and could solve problems, while, today, too often we get students who have only (temporarily) retained a good deal of content in order to pass a test.

School reform and learning reform

There are many efforts today to reform schools, and there are many controversies. Some people want to make our schools better at what they already do: essayist literacy, content literacy, and test literacy. Others want a new paradigm based on problem solving, collaboration, important themes or challenges, the ability to innovate and create, and the ability to understand and deal with complex systems. Some people even want both: the latter for children from affluent backgrounds and the former for poorer kids presumably headed for service jobs.

While people fight over how to reform our schools, a whole new "school system" has arisen. It represents the deepest competition schools have ever had. Young and old people are learning in this new out-of-school system, and they are learning in ways that are radically different from how learning is organized in school (Gee 2004, 2007b, 2007c; Gee & Hayes 2010; Ito *et al.* 2010; Jenkins 2006a, 2006b). Some educators are drawing new ideas for school reform from this new out-of-school system. Others argue that the sort of learning that goes on in this new system could never happen in school, at least not any schools remotely like we have known up to now.

As policy makers, politicians, and educators debate school reform, there has been a massive and sweeping reform not of schools but of learning in society outside of school. This reform has been facilitated by digital media.

The new out-of-school learning system: Passionate affinity spaces

The new learning system, competing today in many respects with our school systems, is learning as part of popular culture. Popular culture is more complex today than it has ever been, as we will soon see (Johnson 2006). Many different things happen in popular culture, good and bad, deep and superficial. Here we want to talk about one type of learning associated with popular culture, a type that is, we argue, complex, deep, and knowledge-producing.

There is no "official" name for this type of learning, so we will have to make one up. We will call it "passionate affinity-based learning." Passionate affinity-based learning occurs when people organize themselves in the real world and/or via the Internet (or a virtual world) to learn something connected to a shared endeavor, interest, or passion. The people have an affinity (attraction) to the shared endeavor, interest, or passion first and foremost and then to others because of their shared affinity.

Just as school is, in one sense, a place or space where people (students and teachers) are "in school" or "at school," passionate affinity-based learning is done in a place or space, what we call a "passionate affinity space," which may be real or virtual or both (Gee 2007c; Gee & Hayes 2010; Hayes & Gee 2010). A passionate affinity space, and the learning that goes on in it, requires some people associated with the space to have a deep passion for the common shared endeavor. It does not require everyone to have such a deep passion, but it does require them to recognize the value of that passion and respect it, in some sense.

Young people learning and playing the video game *Civilization* or playing chess in a club or via the Internet (or some mixture of both) are in a passionate affinity space, if the conditions are right. So, too, are people building and testing robots or model cars in competitions; people writing fan fiction; people designing land, houses, clothes, and furniture for *The Sims* (a video game); people sharing gardening or cooking lessons and expertise; and through almost any endeavor you could name.

What are the right conditions for a passionate affinity space in which people engage in passionate affinity-based learning? Passionate affinity spaces are a type of interest-driven group (Ito *et al.* 2010). (However, we are trying to avoid words like "group" and "community," since in a passionate affinity space and many so-called interest-driven groups, who is "in" the group is not always easy to define. A person who goes once or rarely to a passionate affinity space for resources or "lurks" in it is in the space, but are they in the "group" or "community"? The point is that people are in the space in different ways.) These spaces must have additional features as well.

First, people are associated with them because of their shared endeavor or interest, not because of their "credentials" (e.g. degrees). They can achieve expert status regardless of their official credentials. Such spaces cannot be defined around or restricted to "professionals" in any credentialing or institutional sense.

Second, some people (usually, but not always, around 20 percent) must have a deep passion for the common endeavor, not just a passing interest (Gee & Hayes 2010; Shirky 2008). This passion may be reflected in different ways, such as an extended commitment of time to the interest and space, high levels of production, and so forth. Others in the space will have many different degrees of interest and may come and go in various ways. But they must affiliate with others in terms of the common interest and show that they respect and value the passion that fuels the most active people in the space.

Third, in passionate affinity spaces, everyone can, if they choose, produce (produce knowledge, create things, do things) and not just consume what others have produced. Of course, there can be and usually are standards—high ones—about what counts as good production and people who produce must accept (or seek to negotiate) and meet those standards.

Fourth, in passionate affinity spaces, people sometimes lead and sometimes follow. Some people lead in some situations and others lead in others. Leadership is flexible, and takes different forms, such as managing the site, introducing new ideas and practices, and helping others. People sometimes mentor ("teach") others and sometimes get mentored. Mentoring is flexible.

Fifth, knowledge in the affinity space is "distributed" in the sense that different people know different things and can share that knowledge when necessary. Often the space has good tools and technologies that store and facilitate knowledge. No one person has to or is expected to know everything all by themselves.

Sixth, the affinity space is not closed, though there may be requirements for entry, and takes in newcomers ("newbies"). It refreshes itself. Unlike school, people do not "progress" all at the same pace, age, or "grade." Movement in the space is quite varied; people may focus on one narrow aspect or explore the entire breadth of the interest area, spend as much time as they want on a particular set of skills or practices, and otherwise pursue quite different learning trajectories.

Seventh, affinity spaces are about sharing a common endeavor where people learn things, produce things or knowledge, and can, if they wish, become experts ("professional amateurs" or "pro-ams," see: Anderson 2006; Leadbeater & Miller 2004). Even these experts believe there is always something new to learn, more to discover, and higher standards to achieve.

Passionate affinity spaces are one distinctive type of interest-driven group. People can be nice or mean within them. Some operate quite cordially and collegially and some do not. In some, people flame each other and "haze" newbies (to ensure that they are "tough" enough). Both caring and cruel passionate affinity spaces can produce knowledge and learning. Both are, in that sense, alternatives to our traditional school system. We prefer caring passionate affinity spaces, as we prefer caring schools.

We want to focus now on how learning happens in passionate affinity spaces and how radically this differs from school as we know it. In the rest of this chapter and in the next we turn to video games as one (but only one) area where the new out-of-school learning is apparent.

Early passionate affinity-based learning: The role of "amateurs"

We will delve into some of the main attributes of out-of-school passionate affinity-based learning in the next chapter. In that chapter we will discuss specific examples. This new out-of-school learning system does not require digital media, but digital media were essential to its rapid growth.

Passionate affinity-based learning is not really new. It is just much more widespread today than it has ever been, thanks to digital media. In the eighteenth century and much of the nineteenth century a good deal of scientific discovery occurred through something akin to a passionate affinity space. Many scientists were "amateurs" (Allen 1994; Lucier 2009; Myers 1990). Many did not work for scientific institutions or universities, but "did science" on their own. They supported their research with their own money (as did Darwin and Benjamin Franklin), or they might generate funds by collecting samples for others or giving paid lectures to the public (as did Alfred Russel Wallace, the co-founder of the evolutionary theory).

The amateur scientists kept in contact with others across the world via letters. They shared their discoveries and gained help from others in different countries. They sometimes met face-to-face in official and unofficial meetings, but they may never have seen some of their correspondents. People with different degrees of expertise and of different ages dealt directly with each other. Those with more expertise often welcomed the involvement of newcomers and helped them get started, if the newcomers were sufficiently dedicated.

Science journals in the eighteenth and nineteenth centuries published articles that were written as letters and contained narratives about what the scientist had seen and done (Myers 1990). The more standard scientific "essay" arose as more formal societies for science were organized, began to compete with each other, and as science gradually became a more professional activity (Bazerman 1988). Of course, science eventually became rooted in universities and other institutions, a process that started in the nineteenth century. People who did not have the "right" credentials or work for the right sort of institutions no longer counted as scientists. The "amateur scientist" died out, for the most part.

Another activity that was organized into passionate affinity spaces was "birding" (Weidensaul 2007). People with a passion for finding birds and keeping lists of the birds they saw, by the twentieth century, organized themselves into clubs. They published newsletters that contained members' lists. Expert birders kept in contact by letters, newsletters, and trips to "bird" with each other. They shared knowledge about where to see rare birds. Even very adept birders mentored each other and welcomed interested newcomers. Today birders use phones and the Internet to alert each other to places where interesting or rare birds can be seen.

In the nineteenth and twentieth century, birders competed with ornithologists (with some conflicts) to discover new knowledge about birds and their habits. This is true even today (and rarely in any other area of science), though official "credentials" mean more than they ever have, even in ornithology.

Such early passionate affinity-based learning was reliant on literacy. Letters, lists, and newsletters were crucial for storing and sharing knowledge. Bird guides (books that help birders identify birds) became foundational for modern birding to flourish, just as did binoculars and scopes.

What was true of nineteenth century science and of birding has become commonplace today. Thanks to digital media the reach of passionate affinity-based learning has exploded, and this has meant a return to "amateurs" who compete with professionals (Anderson 2006; Leadbeater & Miller 2004; Shirky 2010). This return of amateur knowledge production is raising questions about the meaning of professional credentials. It has been a long time since "amateurs" like Darwin or Franklin could become world-renowned experts. But that time is returning. In the next chapter we will see "amateurs" (old and young) producing all sorts of knowledge outside the strictures of credentials and institutions.

Complex systems

The nature of expertise and knowledge production has changed in our current world. Today, more than ever in history, humanity faces the perils and possibilities of complex systems. Complex systems have so many variables interacting in such complex ways that it is difficult (or impossible) to predict how the system will behave. When we intervene in such systems there tends to be many unintended consequences, some of them potentially quite disastrous.

Complex systems have always existed. The environment, weather, national economies, as well as the global economy, the rise and fall and clash of civilizations, the growth and interaction of religions, and the spread of viruses are all complex systems. What is new is how humans have intervened in these systems, or created new complex systems, to the point where we are constantly endangered by the unintended consequences of what we do and what we have created.

Many former "natural systems" are today hybrids of nature and human intervention. The heat in Phoenix is now caused by nature (it is a desert after all) and by the "heat island" effect caused by too much concrete storing heat all day and releasing it at night. Global warming is an intricate mix of nature and human intervention and it is hard to disentangle the effects of each (Gore 2006). Our rivers, streams, and oceans are so polluted, overfished, and redirected (by dams, reservoirs, and so forth) that they are no longer "natural" systems. Human global interactions with each other and the environment (e.g. cutting into rainforests, traveling across the world in planes) have exposed us to viruses we have never seen before.

Understanding complex systems requires the work of more than a single lone expert. It requires a team of experts, each with their own specialty, but each capable of understanding the big picture, working with other experts, and creating new interdisciplinary tools, methods, and shared language. The "wisdom of the crowd" (Surowiecki 2004) also plays a role, since the knowledge that diverse sorts of everyday people have, when pooled, can lead to important insights that are beyond even the experts.

A core skill in the new global "knowledge economy" is what we call "system thinking"—being able to think about and work with others to deal with complexity and complex systems. This core twenty-first century skill should by no means be restricted to credentialed professionals. Everyone needs the ability to deal with complexity today.

Competition for schools

We have claimed that out-of-school learning in passionate affinity spaces is competition for schools as we have traditionally thought of them. Learning in these spaces is organized quite differently than in schools. Often people of different ages are together. Different people teach or mentor at different times. The emphasis is on problem solving centered on a shared theme or endeavor, not on "content" derived from a discipline. Finally, passionate affinity spaces often involve systems thinking and other twenty-first century skills not often on offer in schools today. We will close this chapter with a couple of short examples to make clear what exactly we mean.

Our first example is a teenage girl from a rural and working-class family in the Midwest (Gee & Hayes 2010). This girl we will call "Jade." Jade was an average student in school at best. She liked to play video games, and at one point, she played the video game *The Sims*. *The Sims* is a game where the player constructs and maintains a household, a family, and a neighborhood through long periods of time (a lifetime or even generations). It is a simulation of life. It is also the best-selling game in history. One attractive feature of the game is that players can buy or create houses, furniture, clothes, and many other things for the "Sims" (virtual people).

Jade joined an after-school club that was meant to help young women get interested in technology. The club used *The Sims* as one activity, to see if the game could be used as a starting point for fostering an interest in technology among the girls (as computer games seem to do for boys more generally). Jade had stopped playing *The Sims* before joining the club. Though she played the game again as part of the club's activities, she soon lost some of her interest in playing. Instead, she became fascinated by the potential to create clothes from pictures of real clothes, using Adobe Photoshop, and import them into the game for her Sims to wear.

Jade did not know how to do any of this, nor did the people running the club. They told Jade she would need to learn about Photoshop, and directed her to some online tutorials. Jade spent weeks following tutorials on *The Sims* fan sites, learning to use Photoshop (no easy task), and perfecting her ability to create new *Sims* clothing. Making clothes for *The Sims* in this way requires technical knowledge about images, vision (i.e. how to transform images in ways that look realistic), Photoshop, and the underlying source code in *The Sims*. It also requires "taste" and a sense of design.

Jade encountered highly technical and specialist language as she learned to use tools like Photoshop and follow *The Sims* design tutorials. Even the most basic tutorials required that she interpret the names of files and file extensions (such as alpha.bmp and NormalMap.texture.bmp), understand that file extensions refer to different kinds of files that may or may not be modified with different tools (i.e. Photoshop files have PSD extensions and cannot be opened with Bodyshop, a *Sims* tool that requires the use of bitmap [BMP] files). She also had to understand the meaning of terms that related both to tools in Photoshop and to aesthetic features of what she was designing, such as hue, saturation opacity, spread, and noise. Other terminology found in Photoshop and its tutorials were important to the design process itself, such as layer mask, anti-aliased (a property of the image), contiguous (in this case, the areas adjacent to a selected color range), and tolerance. She had to associate icons with different tools and properties of the image she was editing. Often she had to interpret a combination of numeric and textual information: 1024 × 1024 pixels, 100 percent opacity, and so forth.

Jade joined a *Sims* fan site where *The Sims* designers mentored newcomers and where people could upload their creations to let other people use them in their games. She became a better and better designer with help from people on the site. Eventually hundreds of people from around the world downloaded her designs and left notes thanking and praising her. This inspired her to go further.

Jade learned about *Second Life* in her club, a virtual world with content built by its own players, using complicated 3-D design tools that *Second Life* makes available. Most people in *Second Life* just buy what others have designed (houses, developed land, furniture, clothes, cars, and almost anything else you can think of), finding the design process too demanding.

Jade became involved with the teen version of *Second Life*. There, with help from members of that space, she built her own store and designed clothes and other things for *Second Life*. She sold them for "Linden dollars" (*Second Life*'s currency), which are legally exchangeable for "real" money. She began to run her own business and make money.

Jade became interested in technology more generally and became quite adept with computers and software. She earned the respect of her friends, teachers, and the many people she met on *The Sims* fan site and in *Teen Second Life* from across the world. When asked what her experiences had taught her and any influence they had on her goals, she said she had learned that computers give you power and that she wanted to work with computers.

Jade is still not very successful at school. Her school would never really officially acknowledge her growing skills or give her credit for them. When she wanted to take a graphics art class, the school would not let her unless she took a prerequisite course that was, by this time, all "baby stuff" for her. A low grade in a previous math course kept her out of a computer programming course she wanted to take.

Outside of school, Jade learned computational skills, the ability to use different software, the science of transforming images, design skills, entrepreneurial skills (as she ran her business), global communication skills with people across the world, and gained respect and confidence. She learned none of this at school. Her learning out of school, though deeper than school, led to no official credentials. That learning was supported by passionate affinity spaces like *The Sims* fan site and *Second Life*, as well as the club she joined, run by people who well understood passionate affinity-based learning and spaces, as well as the importance of linking young people to them.

The skills Jade learned out of school are arguably more important for her future than much of what she learned in school. Furthermore, her out-of-school learning motivated her desire to learn more at school, though the school refused to let her pursue this interest on her terms. Unfortunately, only school could give her an official credential to "verify" her learning.

Our second story is about Jesse, a Latina woman in her twenties (Hayes & Gee 2010). Jesse did reasonably well in school but struggled in her geometry class. As a young adult, Jesse began playing *The Sims Online*, a multiplayer version of *The Sims* (no longer active). She actually ran a Mafia family in *The Sims Online* for a while. Jesse eventually gravitated to *Second Life*, along with many of her friends from *The Sims Online*. There she then became interested in being a designer, particularly of houses and other environments. One motivation was her desire to create large and attractive spaces for her extended Mafia family (reconstituted in *Second Life*) that had dozens of members.

To design objects for *Second Life* one must use a 3-D design tool that requires knowledge of geometry. After all, objects, houses, and landscapes have parts that must fit perfectly together. The *Second Life* 3-D design tool uses a 3-D grid with x, y, and z coordinates, allowing designers to see the relationship of numeric values to an actual object as they create it. Jesse practiced with this tool for many hours and became a respected designer. She observed that geometry now made sense, because she could actually see what happened to objects when she manipulated their numeric coordinates, even walk through (with her avatar) something she created to experience the result. She now feels quite comfortable with geometry, likes it, and helps other people with it. Furthermore, she is today a graduate student studying educational technology, inspired by her work in *Second Life*.

Jesse learned geometry in *Second Life*, out of school, when it was part of what was called "designing." She acquired a situated understanding of geometric terms and concepts that previously were abstract and meaningless, such as axis, coordinates, coordinate planes, directrix, slope, transversal, vertex, and many others. She did not learn geometry in school when it was called "geometry," she had no purpose for learning it, and there was not a passionate group of people around to help her, respect her, and let her help them.

School "owns" what counts as "literacy" and "knowledge." School "counts" only a narrow range of each. Jade and Jesse picked up new "ways with words" as they became "amateur experts" (that is, experts without credentials). They had to master technical language as they mastered technical practices. They had to master artistic language as well, as they also mastered aesthetic practices. Technical knowledge and artistic knowledge were nowhere near as separate for them as they are in school or in our current obsession (in the United States, at least) with STEM (Science, Technology, Engineering, and Mathematics).

9

PLAY AND THEORY CRAFTING

Video games

There are many examples today of passionate affinity spaces. There are many passionate affinity spaces that are tied to digital media and each one can reveal something different about how learning, knowledge, and socialization are beginning to work together in new ways in the twenty-first century. Here we turn to an example that indicates many of these trends. We will turn to another example in the next chapter.

Our example is centered on the very popular massively multiplayer video game *World of WarCraft* (hereafter *WoW*). We will focus on players who develop a passion for fully understanding the game. Such players engage with each other on web sites to analyze the game, share information about it, modify the game, make new technical tools for the game, and discuss, critique, and reflect on the game.

First we will say a few things about video games and gaming more broadly. Over the last few years there has been a growing interest in video games. This interest has developed partly because the game industry generates so much revenue and so many people play video games. The average age of gamers today is 34 years old (Entertainment Software Association 2010). While more men play than women, a great many girls and women do play and the majority of players of the best-selling game in history, *The Sims*, are girls and women (Lockwood 2007).

The interest in games has arisen also because many policy makers and educators believe that the technology of games, which stresses immersion, interactivity, and problem solving, holds out great promise for making games and other learning devices for purposes other than entertainment (Federation of American Scientists 2006; Gee 2007b, 2007c; Shaffer 2007; Squire 2008). There are already games designed to promote learning, health, understanding of social issues, and other purposes.

A final reason for the interest in video games is that video games have become a major expressive and even artistic force beside their older cousins: books, movies, and television. Many young people (i.e. from their mid-thirties and younger) now devote time to video games that they used to devote to television and to a lesser extent, movies and books (Zane 2005).

There are many different types of video games, games that involve action, adventure, exploration, shooting, building civilizations, playing sports, and engaging in simulations and role-playing of all sorts. To those people who do not play video games, they can be a confusing phenomenon.

We can (roughly) distinguish two large classes of games: casual games and what we will call "world games." Casual games are usually designed around one type of problem, and can be played in short bursts of time. Good casual games are simple to learn but hard to master thoroughly. *Tetris* was one of most famous early casual games and there are now thousands of such games, like *Drop 7*, *Bejeweled*, and *Peggle* (Juul 2009).

World games involve a player manipulating a character, several characters, or even many characters and objects (such as in a "real-time strategy" game like *Age of Empires* or *Rise of Nations*) inside a world with time and space. The game demands that the player solve multiple sorts of problems, much as in real life. Players have to find their way around the world, explore, complete quests or other goals, and usually prevail over some sort of competition. These games can take a long time to finish and often require lengthy play sessions for the player to make meaningful progress. Games like *Half-Life*, *Deus Ex*, *Civilization*, *Spore*, *God of War*, *Call of Duty*, and *WoW* are world games. So-called "arcade games" like *Super Mario Brothers* (and the many related games that have followed) have some elements like casual games, but involve extended play in a changing world.

Games that can be played only by one player are called "single player games." "Multiplayer games" can be played by several players, from two to dozens. Some games (e.g. *Halo*) can be played in single player mode, collaboratively (two players helping each other), or as a multiplayer game (many players both collaborating and fighting against each other). Still other games are "massively multiplayer" games in which thousands of people are playing at any one time (on different servers), any given player can encounter many other players and interact with them (or not) at any time, and any player can group with others in small or large groups to play together (e.g. to accomplish quests or goals as a team).

WoW is what is known as a "massively multiplayer online role-playing game" (MMORPG for short). In *WoW*, thousands of players play together in an enormous and persistent game world (just like in the real world, if you do something in the world, like plant a tree, it will be there forever until something else happens to it). Players develop friendships, fight monsters, and engage in quests that can span hours, days, or weeks.

We will give a brief introduction to *WoW* below. Readers should keep in mind that its designers change *WoW* all the time, making minor and major modifications to the game world and game play. Our description below is meant to give the reader an idea of how complex the game is. Players of the game will need no such introduction and they can skip the next section. Readers unfamiliar with games like *WoW* may find the detail below "overkill" (but, believe us, we are oversimplifying greatly). Just skim the section to get the point that the game is complex and involves players making moment-by-moment decisions about many interacting variables. Readers who want additional information can see the many *WoW* sites on the Internet, such as www.worldofwarcraft.com, www.wowwiki.com, and http://thot-tbot.com.

WoW

WoW is a role-playing game. This means that each player chooses an avatar, a virtual character that the player will play in the world. Players design the avatar's appearance and choose its name. They also make a wide variety of choices about the virtual character's abilities and style of play. Their character is their representative in the game. They will interact with other real people (and their characters) through their character or "avatar."

Players choose whether their avatars will be male or a female. Players choose a "race." Some races are in a confederation called "the Alliance." These races are: Draenei, Humans, Dwarves, Night Elves, and Gnomes. Other races are in a confederation called "The Horde." These races are: Blood Elves, Orcs, Tauren, Trolls, and Undead. Each race has different weaknesses, strengths, and different "racial traits" that give them certain special abilities.

Next a player must choose a "class." The classes in *WoW* are: warriors, mages, druids, death knights, hunters, warlocks, priests, paladins, rogues, and shamans. Classes are like a "profession." Each class has different skills and develops more over time. Therefore, what class the player chooses will affect how the player plays the game. For example, priests can develop considerable skill at healing, among other things. Mages can become quite adept at magic, but cannot fight well with weapons at close quarters (in part because they cannot acquire the most protective armor). Warriors are, on the other hand, very good with weapons at close quarters, though they are not adept at magic.

Players of the same class, for example, two players who have both chosen to be priests, can differentiate themselves by choosing to specialize in one of three different sets of "talents," or skills, each displayed on a "talent tree." Each talent tree contains more than two dozen talents. As players accomplish more quests and goals, they can choose a new skill from any one of the three trees. In theory a player can choose skills from all three trees over time, though players usually specialize in one tree or another, so that they get powerful in one cohesive area of talents (e.g. healing).

A priest, for example, has access to talents in the holy, discipline, and shadow trees. One priest could become a "shadow priest" by specializing in shadow talents (emphasizing the ability to damage enemies), while another could become a "holy priest" by focusing on holy talents (emphasizing the ability to heal), while yet another could become a "discipline" priest (emphasizing the ability to resist damage). Each type of priest will play the game differently and contribute different things to the teams he or she joins. Ultimately any two priests or warlocks or any other class can be quite different in what they can do well and what they cannot.

The talents in the talent trees are not the only skills players can gain. As they play, players also gain abilities to use specific types of weapons and different types of armor. They also can learn skills associated with different "professions," such as skinning animals, mining minerals, creating potions, or making weapons and armor. Players increase their skills by using them (e.g. using particular types of weapons more than others) and by "leveling up," that is, gaining enough experience through successful quests to rise in potential level of power and skill.

Each character of a specific class, and "spec'd out" (i.e, equipped) with certain skills from the talent trees, has many distinctive spells (magic spells that can be cast to do damage, heal oneself or others, give aid of different sorts to others, or cause a number of different effects) and distinctive abilities to use various sorts of weapons and armor in combat in different ways.

Casting a spell or using a weapon requires some sort of finite resource, things like mana, rage, energy, combo points, and so on. For example, casting magical spells requires mana and when mana runs out a player can no longer cast spells until the mana has slowly grown back, or the player's character takes a mana potion, or some other player casts a spell giving the original player his or her mana back. In addition, many spells have cool down and casting times. They take different amounts of time to cast and the cast can be interrupted if the player is attacked while casting a spell. After they have been cast, they must "cool down" for a certain period of time before they can be cast again. Other abilities (like running or fighting with various sorts of weapons) require similar resources, times to take effect, and cool downs.

Different enemies are vulnerable or resistant to various kinds of attacks and require different strategies to be defeated. Players often have to coordinate their actions with other players to kill a powerful enemy or large numbers of less powerful enemies. How much damage a player does over time, often called a player's "damage per second" (DPS), is affected by the player's race, class, skills, armor and other equipment, the speed with which the player casts spells, and a host of other variables. In addition to leveling up and gaining experience points through slaying enemies, players can earn better equipment (dead enemies "drop" equipment sometimes) or gold, which can be used to buy things at auction houses or stores.

Cross-functional teams

Why have we given you all this arcane information? We want you to appreciate, at least a little, how complex the game is and how many decisions players have to make as they play. To understand how to play well, players must consider what their class (e.g. priest or mage) can do well and what it cannot. They have to take into account all the skills they have chosen from the talent trees and how these skills can be integrated. They have to consider all their other skills (e.g. with specific sorts of weapons or damage dealing). They have to be familiar with the equipment they have, the advantages and disadvantages of each item, and how their equipment can be best combined. They have to decide in what order they will cast their spells (their "rotation"), considering the spells' casting times and cool down periods, the potions they have, and the help they can get from others. There is much more that players need to think about, more than we can describe here. In addition, players must often make decisions involving all these variables in microseconds, in the midst of game play, as well as make decisions through reflection before and after play.

These choices become even more complicated when a player is playing with a team, and many *WoW* players spend most of their time playing with teams. The core team structure in *WoW* is a five-person group. Such five-person groups can join other five-person groups and enter "dungeons" (areas with distinctive challenges and rewards) as a much bigger team to fight particularly powerful monsters (some dungeons can take many hours of massive effort and coordination to finish successfully).

Usually, no five-person group is made up of players all in the same class, especially if they have all chosen the same talents from the talent trees. For success in difficult play situations, a team must be balanced; that is, have members who bring together quite different and distinctive skills. A good team has at least one player who is skilled at healing and one or more who are skilled at close combat (classes that excel at close combat are called "tanks" and are capable of giving and withstanding a lot of damage in close encounters). Other players on the team will be from classes that are skilled at fighting from a distance (for example, by casting damaging spells) and at casting helpful "buffs" (temporary beneficial spells or effects) on the other players.

At the more challenging levels of game play, players demand that any team member be very skilled at their class and all its talents. A player must be a proficient specialist. But players also demand that any team member deeply understands the skills and roles of the other classes, so they can integrate their own specialty with the specialties of other players on the team. Many players have "alts," or alternative characters of other classes that they play from time to time to learn how other classes behave and how they can best collaborate with them on a successful team.

Players have to be experts in one specialty, but they must understand the "big picture" and other people's specialties enough to play as a team that is smarter and more powerful than any single player on the team. Ironically, this type of team is very common in today's high-stress, high-tech workplaces. It is called a "cross-functional team" because each member of the team must have a specific function and expertise but must also be able to understand, integrate, and function well with each of the other team members' functions and expertise (e.g. Gee *et al.* 1996; Parker 2002).

For example, in one business project, an engineer, marketing person, manufacturing expert, and shipping coordinator may have to "play together" to create a product better and more quickly than their competition. Companies can no longer wait for each expert to hand off their work to the next expert in a slow chain that often involves sending the product back down the line of expertise to correct errors.

In Chapter 6 we mentioned Alan Greenspan in our discussion of the danger of individual experts' trust in their individual expertise alone. The US and global economy took a major blow because experts like Greenspan operated under the old model of individual experts thinking separately. Greenspan should have been part of a cross-functional team including social scientists, ethicists, psychologists, and experts on complex adaptive systems. A single economist or group of economists trying to predict and control the economy is the equivalent of a single warrior, or group of nothing but warriors, trying to win a dungeon. They could not do anything but tank, and with no one to heal, fight from afar, or use other strategies, they all would die. Greenspan, given his lack of ability to see the big picture and collaborate, would have been thrown out of a *WoW* dungeon.

Theory crafting

It should be clear from our description of *WoW* that it is a complex game and virtual world. In fact, *WoW* is a complex system, in a sense. We argued in the last chapter that complex systems, and the sorts of complex-system thinking they require, are a hallmark of life in the twenty-first century global world.

In *WoW* we see an example of popular culture giving rise to a complex system for people to play in, live in, and study. Many *WoW* players become so passionate about the game, and desire so much to achieve mastery in it, that they become "scholars" of the game. They devote the sort of research and analysis we associate with science to the complex system that is *WoW* (Steinkuehler & Duncan 2008). They do so in a quite modern way, using and creating "smart tools" and collaborating with other experts.

Outcomes of any actions in *WoW* are the result of the interactions of many variables. Complex statistical models determine how these variables interact. The outcome of any action a player takes in battle, for instance, is an outcome of probabilities assigned to numerous interacting variables. Their interaction is complex enough, however, that emergent and unpredictable outcomes are possible. The system is so complex that even its professional designers do not fully understand its dynamics, and they "tweak" (modify) the game continuously to achieve balance among the different classes and different styles of play.

Players who have a passion for studying the game often become expert enough to argue with the professional designers about how the system should be modified. They build tools for the game, as we will discuss below, that millions of players use. These tools range from software that calculates a character's damage per second in a battle to devices that compile information to assist players in making decisions about what to buy and how to price items at the in-game auction house. Blizzard Entertainment, the company that makes the game, allows many of these fan-created "add-ons" to be downloaded and used in the game. Many such add-ons are now essential to game play for countless players.

Players who want to gain expertise in *WoW* often join with others in an intensive sharing of knowledge about the game. They seek to understand its underlying statistical models. They study the best ways to design and play each type of character in different situations. They discover and share new game play strategies. They use highly technical knowledge to design new tools that improve game play and allow players to understand better what they are doing or should do. They are passionate about the game. They engage in passionate affinity-based learning of a deep and highly technical sort.

The study of a game like *WoW* as a system (seeking to understand how its underlying statistical models, variable interactions, and game mechanics work at the deepest level) is called "theory crafting" by the *WoW* community (see, for example, www.wowwiki.com/Theorycraft). Many players use the knowledge they gain from sites devoted to theory crafting to improve their play, and many contribute their own data and analyses to these sites that have become collaborative and communal repositories of knowledge. Such sites also become "schools" to educate newcomers in theory crafting and to allow more expert players to hone their skills and knowledge further. There are, in addition, many other sites devoted to *WoW* that support other types of learning and knowledge building activities, but here we will concentrate on a site devoted to theory crafting called *Elitist Jerks*.

Elitist Jerks is a *WoW* discussion forum focused on the analysis of game mechanics and high-end raiding (in raids, large numbers of players go into special dungeons to fight particularly powerful enemies; successful raids often require a great deal of research, sharing of information, and pre-planning). The name "Elitist Jerks" is not intended ironically. The site has high standards for the format of discussions, and they are quite unapologetic about these standards. The introduction to the site states: "If you feel our rules are stupid or arbitrary, we don't really care. If you don't wish to follow them, you're welcome to return to the official Blizzard forums" (Boethius 2009).

We mentioned in the last chapter that some passionate affinity spaces are caring and some are cruel. *Elitist Jerks* is not cruel—in fact, they demand that all posts are polite and civil—but they are "tough." They demand compliance with the rules. They demand that contributors write clearly and succinctly, write about topics that are new and worthwhile, not ask questions that have already been answered, search and read before posting, engage in research and analysis, and not engage in "whining" (complaining). The site's rules say: "If you have an idea you'd like to share with the community, support it with analysis, testing, or both that indicates you've put some thought into it" (Boethius 2009). Sounds like a good school, indeed.

Damage per second (DPS)

One issue that concerns high-end *WoW* players is their "damage per second" (DPS). Some of the higher-end guilds in *WoW* demand that players achieve the highest possible DPS in raids. How much DPS a player achieves depends on many interacting variables, such as the player's (character's) race, class, equipment ("gear"), skills (of which each player has dozens), "buffs" (helpful spells cast on a player), and the speed and order with which the player uses spells.

Here is one post from *Elitist Jerks* meant to help players understand DPS at a deep and technical level. This post is long and highly technical, and we will look at only a small part of it. Here is what the post says just about melee damage, that is, fighting in close combat (Binkenstein & Malan 2008):

- Average weapon damage (A) can be calculated by adding the high and low ends of the damage range, then dividing by two.
- Weapon DPS is calculated by taking the average damage and dividing by the weapon speed (S).

$$DPS = \frac{A}{S}$$

- Crits—Melee crits are a chance to add 100% of the weapon damage. To add damage from critical hits the average damage is multiplied by the Crit percentage (C).

Below is what the post says about doing damage by casting spells. In this quote, "DoT" means "damage over time" (spells often do damage for a certain period of time after they are cast), HPS means "healing per second" (priests and some other classes can cast healing spells, spells that restore life points over time), and DD means "direct damage" (which usually refers to any type of magic spell whose direct effect is to cause burst damage—loss of life points—to one or multiple targets).

- Average spell damage is calculated the same way as weapon damage (high + low divided by two) for direct damage spells. DoT spells do not have damage ranges.
- Spell DPS (or HPS) is calculated by taking the damage divided by the cast time. DoT spells are calculated by taking the total damage divided by the total DoT duration. You may also want to include the cast time if there is no direct damage portion of the spell.
- DD + DoT spells will be DD/cast + DoT/duration.
- Spell crits—The chance to add 50% damage to a hit. To get the extra damage from spell crits, multiply the average damage by the Crit % and 0.5 (plus any talent/item Crit bonus modifier).
- Spell damage—This is a bonus to the damage of spells, for details on the co-efficient calculations, see the [Article]Spell Coefficients[/Article] article .

There is no need for the reader to understand any of this. Our point is that these excerpts are a formal analysis of a small aspect of DPS, itself only one small part of game play, based on a player's own research. We emphasize that this kind of analysis is now common. Entering "theory crafting" (or "theorycrafting") for *WoW* will bring up hundreds of thousands of hits on Google, many even more technical than the quotes above.

There are a number of points to make about theory crafting. First, a company (Blizzard) has created a complex system and its players study it using scientific and mathematical ways of thinking, as well as highly specialized uses of language. Yet it is not a complex system in the "real" world. Should we bemoan that these skills are being applied to a "play" system and not a "real world" one?

Second, these players are developing and using technical, technological, scientific, mathematical, research, analysis, collaboration, and argumentative skills that are the skills we hope people develop in school and that are central to work and life in the global, high-tech, complex-system-ridden twenty-first century. In this sense, the players' research is relevant to the real world.

Third, many people engaged in this research are amateurs. They need not, and many do not, have any official credentials in statistics, science, or computer science. Indeed, some are still in high school. On some sites such people engage with the professional game designers who designed and maintain *WoW*, arguing with them and contesting who has the best theory about how the game works or should work. In general, the amateurs are treated with respect by the professionals.

Fourth, this is very much a collaborative and community effort. Theory crafters discuss their work with each other and build on each other's work, sometimes disputing and contesting results, across the globe on fan-based Internet sites like *Elitist Jerks* and a great many others. Science itself is collaborative and communal, as well as competitive, so these players are engaged in a process resembling how actual scientists work.

Fifth, these theory crafters are not supported by any official institutions. They maintain their own standards internally. Participation is determined by interest, passion, and willingness to follow the rules. People of quite different ages and degrees of expertise can be present. People can contribute a lot or a little. They can largely consume or they can produce knowledge.

Sixth, there are many different sites devoted to theory crafting and other *WoW* related activities. Players have many choices. As *Elitist Jerks* says, if someone does not like their rules, there are other places they can go, including to official forums sponsored by Blizzard. Or they could start their own site.

Seventh, what these "amateurs" do affects how people play the game and, thus, affects Blizzard, the company that makes the game. We will discuss below how player-made "mods" affect game play in significant ways. A company like Blizzard will change aspects of the game based on what players are saying and discovering about it. In a sense, the players are (free of charge) designing and re-designing the game and the way it is played. They are taking a certain type of "ownership" over the game.

Eighth, learning happens in a very interesting way in passionate affinity spaces like ones devoted to *WoW* theory crafting. Learners can enter these spaces at any level of experience and be of different ages. They learn by joining a knowledge-producing community. They can learn in many different ways, for example, through tutorials, discussion, their own research and problem solving, or didactic instruction offered by others. Their learning is in constant relation to game play, which motivates that learning and through which they can see in practice how what they have learned works. They are testing their hypotheses, theories, and what they have learned through tests or experiments in the game all the time.

Elitist Jerks is a passionate affinity space. People of different ages and degrees of expertise are there because they have an interest in perfecting their *WoW* game play and knowledge. A smaller number of these people have a deep passion (beyond mere interest) for theory crafting and everyone must respect that passion as the central "attractor" of the space. In the space, people create tools to support play and learning. They consume and produce knowledge. They collaborate and innovate. They need have and ask for no professional credentials (though nothing stops a professional from entering).

Learning in school could resemble passionate affinity spaces, save for the institutional inertia of schools. To support such learning, schools as we know them would have to disappear and society would have to adopt a different paradigm of schooling. Passionate affinity spaces exist out of school where people are learning all sorts of things. For example, many young people are learning to write on fan fiction sites. They are also learning English and other languages on such sites (Black 2008). Other people are learning science, robotics, design, business, ecology, graphic art, cooking, birding, engineering, and many other things in such spaces. Within such spaces people have the opportunity to become lifelong learners, designers, and knowledge producers. Their learning is always preparation for future learning, not for "tests" of the sort we use in school.

There is an equity problem with this out-of-school learning. In principle it is open to everyone. In principle, everyone has a chance, if they want, to be passionate and be a top producer in the space. But, new data suggest that much of the higher-end knowledge production in many passionate affinity sites is done by more privileged young people, not as much by poorer ones (Hargittai 2010). If these are, as we think, sites for learning twenty-first century skills, this is a problem. Of course, this is the same problem we have had with literacy learning in our schools: more privileged children learn to read and write better than do many poorer children.

Mods

Many video games today are sold with a version of the software with which they were made. This software allows players to modify the game in small or large ways. They can make new environments, design new levels, or even make whole new games. For example, in the popular series of *Tony Hawk* skateboard games, players can make new skate parks and design their own skateboarders, skateboards, and skating tricks (and assign them points in the game). Such gamer-made modifications are called "mods."

WoW players use the term "mod" in a somewhat different way. Some *WoW* players design technical tools to make game play easier or more enjoyable. These mods are posted on fan sites, so other players can download them into their games.

As we stated earlier, some player-made mods are used widely and have become essential to game play in *WoW* for many higher-end players.

There are many different types of mods. For example, there are mods that notify priests (and other characters with good healing skills) when to heal other characters in a hunting party or raid. The priest does not have to keep close watch on everyone else's "life bars" to see when they are low enough (from damage) that their characters need healing.

Another interesting mod is one called *DrDamage*. This mod does, as one review says:

> all of your in-game theory crafting for you. It will work the actual values for your damage, +spell damage and +healing based on your gear and talents. It will display the average damage or healing done by a spell on the action bar.
>
> Having an in-game calculator that takes into account your talents and gear is a powerful tool. It's like having your favorite numbers-player sitting next to you all the time. (If you're not that person.) It is certainly a good way to get a feeling of which of your spells or abilities is outputting the most damage or healing. (Forsgren 2008)

Yet another type of mod is a "damage meter." This mod actually solves a major problem in human society, the so-called "free rider" problem. In any group activity there is always the danger that someone will be a "free rider," doing little, letting others do the heavy lifting, and still getting the rewards for the group's efforts.

A damage meter—and there are many different versions—allows players to display on the screen, for all to see, a small chart that shows the damage (DPS) done by each member of the group, given their class, gear, and abilities. While *DrDamage* provides a player with his or her own data, a damage meter allows everyone to see how each member of the group is performing. Players who know the game well can readily tell whether each player is doing his or her job and doing it well. A player playing a warrior should be doing lots of damage (more depending on their gear and other things). A player playing a healing priest (i.e. a priest that has chosen many healing skills out of the talent trees) should be doing no damage and plenty of healing.

Damage meters are based on an analysis of the underlying statistical models that drive game play in *WoW*. As you might expect, different players have different opinions about the best analysis to serve as a basis for damage meter calculations. In turn, they argue about which damage meter is most accurate, that is, which one best accounts for all the interacting variables that determine how much damage a given character is doing over time.

Mods of this type demonstrate how players, usually within passionate affinity spaces, are transforming how others play and think about a game. They give everyone additional tools for reflecting on the game and how it functions as a system, while they are playing it and afterwards. Such mods can also facilitate collaboration and integration of cross-functional teams in the game.

Theory crafting and language

Digital media deliver knowledge and language, just like writing and print do. But they do so faster, more widely, more easily, and in a way that allows rapid modification and wider participation. In the end, they greatly enhance a function that literacy already had: the proliferation of specialized knowledge and language (Gee & Hayes 2010). Digital media also change our conception of experts, professionals, and institutions. Does anyone, for example, think that a college organized as a plethora of passionate affinity spaces devoted to academic knowledge and complex systems, spaces with everyone in them (faculty and students alike), would not be as good as or better than many, perhaps all, of our current colleges?

WoW, like any cultural product, will someday go out of date and be replaced by another product. However, the desire that "everyday people" of all sorts have to deeply understand, to gain mastery, to master technical thinking and languages for themselves, and to redesign what they use and the games they play (and even the workplaces within which they work) will not cease. It is a thirst quenched by *WoW* and many other popular culture activities today. In the end, it teaches people to be proactive learners and producers of their own knowledge, core twenty-first century skills.

10

CATS, PASSION, AND EXPERTISE

Complex cats

In this chapter, we illustrate some key themes we have discussed earlier by looking at a listserv devoted to cat health issues. The topic of cat health may seem odd. But that is *the* point: today, people can organize learning, knowledge production, and social interaction with distant others around *anything* (Gee & Hayes 2010).

We live in an age where people are as liable, or more so, to put energy into a personal passion, for example, writing vampire romance stories, cats, or designing clothes for "little people" (virtual people) in *The Sims* as they are to put energy into civic causes in their country or the world. These passionate affinity spaces are, in some respects, new civic spaces composed of people from all over a country or the world.

What drives someone to participate in a site devoted to cats and cat health or any specialist site? Often they want to find others who are the "same" as them, and understand them, not in terms of identities based around class, ethnicity, gender, or job, but around a shared interest or passion that others may find odd or "obsessive." There are many people in the world, so even an obscure or arcane issue can attract the attention of a large number of people from across the world. Digital media's ability to pool people from across a country or the globe allows even very narrow issues and perspectives to achieve audiences, interactions, and influence of a size they never could have before (Shirky 2010).

Cat health also has personal significance for us and, again, this is typical. In a previous book (Gee & Hayes 2010), we argue that very often it is a personal and even seemingly "small" issue or problem that brings people to a passionate affinity space for help. In some cases, they get "hooked" on the space itself and learning within it. Their interest widens, they develop a real passion, and go on to achieve new skills.

Close to three years ago, a young stray cat trotted across our backyard and joined us for dinner as we were eating on our patio. After dinner, he decided to adopt us and moved in. We named him Bandit because of his black face markings. About a month later, we adopted another young cat, Natasha, from a local shelter. She was a delightful, playful little cat who had grown up in shelters and had experienced a rather severe, but common, respiratory illness prior to our adoption. Natasha had a clean bill of health when we adopted her, but within a couple of weeks she developed a fever and enlarged lymph nodes. Thus we began what turned out to be a long and at times overwhelming foray into the world of cat health care.

With the help of an antibiotic, Natasha rapidly became lively and playful again. She seemed healthy, but her lymph nodes remained oddly enlarged. The vet ran tests for every conceivable illness but the results were uniformly negative. Over the course of three years, she was prone to illnesses that briefly slowed her down but that were quickly remedied with medication. Throughout, her lymph nodes stayed enlarged, sometimes changing in size a bit but never shrinking back to normal.

After some early rounds of inconclusive tests, we asked a relative who breeds and shows Maine Coon cats for advice. While she was just as baffled as our vet about Natasha's case, she recommended that we join a couple of online discussion groups devoted to cat health to see if we could locate any information that might be relevant to Natasha's condition. While we never did find a diagnosis, these groups became an invaluable source of other information and, in addition, a fascinating example of how digital media—in this case, a now very "old-fashioned" Yahoo groups listserv—served as a medium for allowing people to access and pool dispersed knowledge, talk across professional boundaries, collectively interpret and question research findings, and at the same time provide emotional and social support.

This, too, is typical these days: the scientific and the technical meet the personal and the social. We seek specialized information in the same place and at the same time we seek social interaction and emotional support. It is also clear that this trend demands, perhaps ironically, a good deal of literacy skills and a tolerance for specialized, complex language. The formal and the informal, distance and solidarity, meet.

fanciershealth

Here we will focus on the list, fanciershealth, a quite active list with more than 4400 subscribers that was founded in 2000. Although the list is designated as a forum for the discussion of pedigreed cats and many of the participants are indeed breeders, there is no restriction on who may join the group. Participants often refer to cats adopted from shelters as well as purebreds.

At first we viewed the list as a sort of database, doing searches with descriptors like "enlarged lymph nodes" in the forum archives and perusing the extensive set of documents and links stored on the group site. We also subscribed to the list, initially with the idea of simply monitoring posts for any mention of a syndrome similar to Natasha's.

Quickly, however, other topics caught our interest and we became avid readers of all messages. Who knew that some feline vaccines could cause sarcoma, that there is a feline version of HIV that causes great concern among cat owners, or that mother cats who have only one kitten in a litter may try to abandon it, since the expenditure of effort to raise a single kitten is not worthwhile in evolutionary terms compared to getting pregnant again, hopefully with a larger litter?

This is a typical progression in a passionate affinity space. We moved from a specific and personal concern to an intense interest in the space and its knowledge more generally. We moved from "everyday knowledge" to more technical knowledge without formal instruction or professional degrees or credentials.

Solidarity and science

One intriguing aspect of this group is the variety of topics discussed and their variation in technicality. As an example, on the day we wrote this section, there were posts on the use of Revolution (a flea control medicine) with pregnant cats and kittens; the pros and cons of feeding the same food to kittens and adult cats; how to identify the reason for a kitten's poor coat and constant retching; the recall of a canned cat food due to inadequate thiamine levels; the treatment protocol for Strep G (a virus that can kill kittens); finding an ointment used for skin problems; possible diagnoses for a cat who was overgrooming; clarifying whether FeLV (feline leukemia) is a core vaccine for kittens; how to handle two cats who were "no longer friends"; and an update on a kitten who was not eating.

Similar to most listservs, the posts were often conversational and informal. However, this informality was intermingled with much more formal language related to scientific research, the nature of diseases, and medications. The discussion of Strep G offers some good examples. For instance, in response to a member who posted a question about the protocol for Strep G, after losing kittens to it, one woman wrote:

> It's not just Strep G that can cause this type of problem. Mycoplasma and E. coli are also implicated, and perhaps something else entirely that is a slow grower in the labs … I told my vet that I just wanted to cry when he told me that the bacteriologist at Cornell allowed that maybe what they grew out wasn't the real problem, but instead just the organism that grew quickest.

And another, in response to a question about whether the original poster had overlooked anything in the literature on Strep G:

> Yup a whole lot of research that has been repeated in clinical practice for a decade or more … Clindamycin is the drug of choice for treating Strep G infections. Safe for pregnant and lactating queens, and neonates. Effective prophylaxis as well as treatment.

Yet even in the posts with more formal language, as the first example above illustrates ("I told my vet that I just wanted to cry"), the writers typically made an effort to include bonding language that "softened" the tone of their message and conveyed their concern and empathy for the problem. Of course, a good veterinarian would likely use similar bonding language in a face-to-face conversation, though it's actually less likely that a vet would discuss research or use the type of formal discourse in the posts above with a pet owner, since they would assume the owner would not understand this "specialist" language. This "democratization" of professional knowledge is made possible in part by the potential of digital technology to create personal connections among professionals and laypeople as well as to give laypeople access to scientific documents that previously were available only to a few (i.e. people with access to a university library or who could attend professional conferences).

Access to this knowledge creates some challenges, however. People must learn to talk about this information in ways that don't distance them from each other, since a significant function of listservs like fanciershealth is to create bonds and provide support to participants as they deal with the emotional aspect of treating their cats' illnesses. They also need help in interpreting and evaluating this information. The list not only helps participants locate and make sense of scientific information, it gives them access to collective experiential knowledge that prior to the Internet would have been difficult or impossible to obtain.

Dispersed knowledge and the filter of collective experience

One purpose of the fanciershealth group is to serve as a sort of clearinghouse for information on cat health-related topics. Just as with almost any topic, the Internet has made a wealth of cat health information available to the average person, information that previously would have been accessible only to vets or through extensive library research.

In addition to compiling information, the list served the crucial purpose of helping participants make sense of all this information. Often in schools the emphasis is on teaching children as individuals who must store everything in their own heads. Groups like fanciershealth suggest that it may be just as important for people to learn how to leverage the communal knowledge available in online affinity spaces. By bringing together the dispersed, local, and specific knowledge of individual members, the list became a sort of filter for screening ideas and illuminating relevant considerations when making decisions about cat care. This is a type of "wisdom of the crowd" (Surowiecki 2004) where knowledge is pooled among a diverse array of people and sources.

One example of such a discussion is a recent exchange about vaccinations. While getting appropriate shots for your cat might seem like a relatively straightforward topic, there is considerable uncertainty over the efficacy of some vaccines and concern over their potential side effects. Indeed, we learned enough about some of these concerns to question whether Natasha, with a potentially compromised immune system, should receive the set of vaccines recommended for 2-year-old cats. When we raised these concerns with our vet—a conversation we would never have had without information from the list—she agreed that Natasha should not be vaccinated. Prior to joining the listserv, we would not have even realized that vaccinations could be negotiable.

The logic of state laws that require rabies vaccinations in particular was debated on the site in light of the relative rarity of rabies infections from pets among humans in the USA. Because the pool of participants was so wide, several people were able to share examples of pets who had not been vaccinated and due to state law had to be euthanized after biting a child or were saved only after lengthy lawsuits. Others reported cases where infected bats had been found in areas where cats also roamed. Many people did not know that state laws about rabies vaccinations could differ (we didn't), and this point led to a lively discussion of differences in laws and their relative merits. Several people argued that they should lobby their state governments for more reasonable regulations, based on what they learned from the discussion.

In addition to sharing information about differences in rabies laws across states, participants also discussed the relative efficacy of rabies vaccines, in this case drawing on scientific research, though they were not trained as researchers or even as veterinary scientists. "Everyday" uncredentialed people engaged in scientific specialist language, as in the quote below where a participant discussed the difference between immunization by injection versus transdermal methods (the vaccine is delivered across intact skin with a high-pressure pump), using FeLV as an example:

> there is a distinct advantage to the transdermal vaccine. By going through the skin the vaccine comes into contact with many more dendritic cells which are VERY immunogenic. That means they can use less volume of vaccine and get a terrific immune response to it. More importantly, the transdermal rFeLV vaccine is the ONLY FeLV vaccine that gives good cell mediated immunity (CMI). Since FeLV is a virus that infects cells, the CMI is very beneficial for protecting against disease. Here is what Dr. Ford says of it on his website (www.dvmvac.com)

In addition to sharing and interpreting medical knowledge, participants shared personal experience as an additional source of information in making judgments about feline health care practices. This pooling of experience at times led to significant differences of opinion, but offered participants a wider range of perspectives. A passionate affinity space allows enough people to aggregate so that there will be a sufficient number of people who have had even relatively rare experiences which allows the space to pool knowledge about rare situations beyond what was possible even in scientific research before the Internet.

For example, one of the concerns about rabies vaccinations in particular was the possibility of a vaccine-related sarcoma (cancer). The possibility of such sarcomas, though rare, has led to a practice of injecting the vaccine in a cat's leg, rather than the previously standard location on the cat's back (so if a sarcoma does develop, the cat can be saved by amputating its leg). The site had enough people who had experienced this rare condition that they carried on a lively debate about vaccine-related sarcomas and shared knowledge that would have been previously very hard indeed to find and pool.

While access to such a wide range of dispersed knowledge has been made possible by the Internet, as well as personal communication with people who share common interests yet are separated geographically, people have of course always relied on the experience of friends and relatives when making decisions. Even when professional advice and knowledge is available, we still turn to people "like us" who can "speak from experience."

A difference in this case is that the list participants were able to consult "strangers" who had more relevant experience than people with whom they had closer personal relationships. They still valued and shared knowledge gleaned from scientific sources and their veterinarians, but the combined experience available through the list offered a useful means of not only interpreting this knowledge, but changing their relationship to veterinary professionals.

Sites like fanciershealth allow the new information typical of weak ties (interactions with people we do not know well and with whom we do not share much local experience) and the socialization and bonding typical of strong ties (interactions with friends and family who share a lot of local experience with us). Such "strong weak" ties, which we discussed in Chapter 5, are typical of passionate affinity spaces.

Relationships with veterinarians: Pro-am meets interpretation police

Apart from the general interest of the subject matter, the discussions also were intriguing because of the participants' critical stance toward many common professional veterinary practices. While most participants were very respectful toward veterinarians in general, often people wrote in to get second opinions if they had reason to question a vet's recommendation or treatment. Sometimes these questions prompted more lengthy discussions of controversial topics, often with reference to scientific research as well as personal experience.

While a common recommendation on the list was to "see your vet" when someone reported a serious problem with their cat, the participants tended to characterize their relationships with their vets as a partnership or collaboration, not as that of a professional–client or expert–novice. Some people described instances of clear ignorance or poor practice on the part of veterinarians, but many offered examples of how they worked together with their vets, using the list as an additional source of information in areas where the vet's knowledge might be incomplete. Here are some examples:

> When using a human drug for animals, this is called "off label use." My vet often asks me to check with my fanciershealth friends for suggested dosages of off-label usage drugs. She also checks her books, and we arrive at the dose she wants me to use.

> Vets do not take as much pharmacy instruction as do actual pharmacists, and it pays to be right on critical dosages for Rx'es of meds that your vet orders infrequently. I'd rather ask the people on this list to be sure of the right dosage amounts, than just blindly do what my vet tells me to do, especially if the numbers seem out of norm.

> I love my vet, he's wonderful. But he's a rural vet in a poor county where animals generally get short shrift. I'll often get drug names and dosages from this list, print them out, then take to him with the cat in question and we can sit and look at the recommendations and see if he agrees or doesn't.

> He'd never heard of using a nebulizer with antibiotics for kittens with upper respiratory problems, but thanks to the info on this list we have, and with great success.

> It was this list that empowered me to take care of my cats and kittens in an intelligent, informed manner. But we should all be aware that as impressed as we might be with this list and/or vets … there is a lot of MIS-information and it should all be backed up with your own research.

On the other hand, some participants raised concerns about relying on the list for information on topics such as medication dosages and other critical issues:

> I'm amazed how many people ask for critical veterinary advice on these lists and take people they don't know and have never met at their word without knowing that person's qualifications.

This comment illustrates a core tension in knowledge-sharing online: while lists such as fanciershealth open up access to other people's experience and insights that were not readily available prior to the Internet, without any way to independently verify that person's experience and credibility, how do you know they are trustworthy? Of course, this is exactly the concern that was raised about writing and books as they proliferated thanks to print.

As the above comments indicate, many of the participants were quick to acknowledge that any advice offered on the list should be verified with additional research and consultation. So why bother using the list at all? After all, there are other "professional" sites that compile information about cat health with presumably more verifiable credentials (we have consulted many of them ourselves, such as the sites sponsored by the Cornell Feline Health Center and the Winn Feline Health Foundation).

One reason is that breeders and passionate owners of multiple cats have particular sorts of expertise, based on the nature of their practices; not only do they deal with many more cats than the average pet owner, they have considerable experience with issues associated with cat fertility, pregnancy, birthing, and raising kittens.

Indeed, back to our personal situation, when we recently decided to adopt a new kitten, we turned immediately to the list to check people's opinions on how old a kitten should be when it leaves its mother, and as a result, we let our kitten stay with its mom for several weeks longer than we—or the breeder—originally planned (and we were surprised that the breeder, though she is only breeding her pet cats, didn't realize she should keep the kittens longer). This collective knowledge was viewed as a significant resource by site members:

> I have been breeding for 10 years and there are many others who have been doing this longer than me. ... As a breeder my feeling is that because I have dealt with cats exclusively that in many cases I feel that I do know more than most veterinarians about feline illness & treatment. Many vets do not deal with cats on a regular basis or do not keep up with continuing education to know about leading cutting edge treatments and medications. Or they are so "anti-breeder" that they refuse to work with us at all.

Despite the stories of collaboration among breeder and vet, as the last comment suggests, there were also accounts of vets who were uncooperative, resented breeders' attempts to participate in their cats' diagnosis and treatment decisions, and generally tried to maintain clear distinctions between their professional knowledge and the "amateur" knowledge of pet owners and breeders. Some participants speculated that this was because they asked too many questions and took up too much time; others pointed out the profit motive as well as the need for vets to protect themselves from liability.

This, too, is indicative of issues in the digital world more generally. The old notion of expertise based on credentials and professional practice is being challenged. At the same time, credentialed professionals are trapped in work models that do not allow them time for wide interactions, sharing with amateurs, engaging with the wisdom of the crowd, or ceding expertise to people with experience but no credentials. But, then, too, passionate affinity spaces can sometimes become so ideologically committed that they splinter and drive out dissenting views.

Intimate strangers

Natasha was a brave and resilient kitty, but at age three she eventually succumbed to her disorder. We were heartbroken in a way that only other cat lovers could understand. We shared our feelings with a few people whom we knew would be sympathetic, but we still felt isolated in our grief. We were also worried about Bandit, who had been devoted to Natasha and wandered the house looking for her.

The list turned out to be a genuine source of emotional support. We found a thread that started with a post from a woman who wanted advice on helping her 14-year-old cat cope with the death of his companion cat. There were 20 replies, full of advice, sympathy, and touching stories of other grieving cats and humans, ranging from a kitten who stopped eating and drinking when his aged "mentor" cat died, to an older cat who sat for days in a travel crate he had shared with his deceased sister cat, waiting for her to return.

We were encouraged by the posts to get a new cat within a few days of Natasha's death, with the perspective that we were not replacing her, but rather making a home for a new and unique personality. We wound up adopting a cat with a striking resemblance to Natasha, and even this experience was echoed in the list. While some people argued against adopting cats that looked similar to the deceased cat, to avoid comparisons with the original, others shared stories of adopting "look-alike" cats with great success and happiness.

Yes, these are people we don't know, and will likely never meet, or even communicate with directly. But hearing just a little about their experiences was a real comfort. The language used in these posts was quite different from the distancing, scientific language interwoven into discussions like those we cited above. Some of the writers referred to distinctly unscientific concepts, like soul mates and a cat shedding "real" tears. While people on the list argued over the validity of scientific research, no one questioned these posts. In this case, closeness and solidarity far outweighed concerns over this type of content. The following post captures some of the personal and supportive nature of this thread:

> My husband and I have almost always gotten a new kitten shortly after losing one of our cats. Of course that kitten cannot be a "replacement" for the one we lost. But we look at it this way: A new kitten forces one to laugh, to pay attention to its antics, to take care of it and carefully introduce it to the family. We still mourn the one we lost—often for years and years. And the terrible thing about it is that my husband noticed some years ago that it was even more fun to get TWO kittens and watch them play. That tends to build up the population a little too much though. LOL
>
> But you can't be in tears all day when a tiny, furry little badness is demanding your love.

We decided to adopt a kitten too.

11

THE RETURN OF THE AMATEUR AND THE NEW CAPITALISM

Early science and amateurs

Earlier in the book we argued that literacy led to institutions as we now know them. Now we will address some foundational questions about institutions: Why do we have them? What are they good for? Why are they weakening today under the forces of digital media? Why are so many people today willing to produce, design, learn, mentor, and share in passionate affinity spaces without necessarily receiving any financial rewards?

Literacy did not give rise to institutions in one fell swoop or all by itself. Literacy gave rise first and foremost to "wide networking." In an oral culture, people's "networks" were usually made up of strong ties, that is, ties to people who they knew well. Such people are not often the source of new or rare information. Within such networks, any one person's impact and influence usually was not very widespread (unless, of course, he or she had an army).

Consider Socrates and Plato. As far as we know Socrates did not write. His influence was through oral dialogue with others. We know his ideas today because Plato did write and wrote down dialogues Socrates had with others. Of course, we can never be sure how much Plato recorded of what Socrates actually said and how much he made up himself.

Plato was by no means the first writer in Western or Greek culture, but he was relatively early in the history of writing in the West and in Greece. He was one of the West's first truly great literary writers (e.g. his *Symposium* is still a literary classic about love). Even so, Plato did not trust writing (Burger 1980: Gee 2007a; Havelock 1976), as we have mentioned before.

Plato thought writing would lead to the destruction of human memory (in many ways it did). He thought literacy would enable people to claim knowledge that they did not really have (it did). He thought writing's capacity to travel far and wide, beyond the control of its author ("father"), meant a text would be abused by readers who did not interpret it the way the author intended (as all authors well know, this too is true).

Plato was also an elitist. He believed people were born with different inherent degrees of intelligence and worth. Only the "best" should be allowed to rule. He supported the idea of "philosopher kings" (of course, he was a philosopher).

Plato had a school where he walked around the gardens instructing his students in philosophy (in those days philosophy and science were not separate enterprises). He shared his written works with his students and peers, but did not want these texts to be taken away and fall into the hands of others, especially people who were not of the highest caliber. Luckily for us, Plato failed in this last goal. His written work has circulated for centuries across the world and is still readily available today (Guthrie 1986; Hare 1982; Havelock 1976; Taylor 2001; Williams 1999).

Plato had a wider network of influence because of literacy. Initially he restricted that network to those people with whom he had personal contact and could monitor through talk and interaction. He kept his network small on purpose.

Monks in the so-called "Dark Ages" kept the ideas of Greece and Rome alive by copying, studying, and storing ancient manuscripts, some by Plato and Aristotle (Plato's best student). By the Renaissance, universities flourished and writing circulated more widely at least to "elites" who could read and sometimes write.

Modern science arose as people like Copernicus, Vesalius, and Galileo in the sixteenth and seventeenth centuries, and later Descartes, Newton, and Leibniz in the seventeenth and eighteenth centuries spread their ideas and influence through papers, books, and letters that kept them in contact with other scientists throughout the world. They challenged the idea of the ancients that truth was determined by authority, religion, or state power and argued it should be determined by empirical evidence. Their networks were wide and their degree of impact and influence large. Newton, however, still kept many of his writings secret, especially those on occult and theological topics (Westfall 1993).

Newton held a position at Cambridge University, but he had other positions in society, as well. He was elected Lucasian Professor of Mathematics in 1669 (Stephen Hawking held this chair until his retirement in 2009). He was also a Member of Parliament and Master of the Mint, a government position (Westfall 1993).

While a scientist like Newton had a network that stretched across a number of countries, it was still in many respects restricted. It was restricted for two reasons. One reason was that handwritten letters and papers traveled slowly (in those days very slowly indeed). Documents were also, in those days, hard to reproduce in large numbers. Printing made it possible to make more copies, but in those days it was still a slow process in terms of production and distribution. Books were not widely available for a second reason: writing and reading, especially about topics like philosophy and science (Newton wrote about both), were restricted to a small number of elites, usually people who were (though not always) well born and well educated. Literacy, as well as education, was not widespread in society.

In the centuries that followed Newton, as we discussed in an earlier chapter, scientists were often "amateurs" who did not engage in scientific activities for money or as part of an official institutional affiliation. Darwin, for instance, never held an academic position, and he did not share his writing very readily or widely beyond his circles of friends and colleagues. He rushed his theory of natural selection into print only when Alfred Russel Wallace was about to co-opt his discovery (Bowler 1990).

In the nineteenth century, science and medicine were often advanced through the circulation of letters within a network of colleagues across a country or several countries (Myers 1990). Doctors (who often had no formal training, but had apprenticed to another doctor) published articles in medical journals that resembled the letters they sent to their peers: stories about a specific experience they had had with a patient (Star 1989; Starr 1982).

Institutions

Why did all this change? Why did amateurs, letters, and narratives disappear? One core reason was a growing belief in the need for standardization to overcome the limitations of individual observations (Myers 1990; Shapin & Schaffer 1985; Star 1989). Amateur naturalists, for instance, made observations and reported them to others in letters, papers, and books, believing that pooled observations from different people would converge on the "truth." This did not prove to be the case.

Observation was not as easy and straightforward a way to gain and pool knowledge as people had thought. Different observers could see the same thing in different ways, often not agreeing on what they had seen or how to interpret what they had seen. Itiel Dror, a psychologist who has studied eyewitness testimony, has said: "The mind is not a passive machine. Once you believe in something—once you expect something—it changes the way you perceive information and the way your memory recalls it" (Grann 2010: 52). The same phenomenon applies to science.

Observation was a problem in early laboratory physics (Shapin & Schaffer 1985). When people ran experiments, they did not always agree on the outcome or what it meant. The same thing happened in medicine. Doctors and surgeons claimed to see different symptoms or even body parts, and interpreted what they saw quite differently.

There was clearly a need for something or someone to vet, norm, and standardize scientific observations. Science became more and more about developing theories, methods, and tools to tame and control diverse observations and interpretations. These theories, methods, and tools, in turn, were monitored by institutions that began to train and evaluate "professionals." For example, medical schools arose to train doctors and medical researchers in established theories, methods, and tools in medicine (Star 1989; Starr 1982). Such education needed to be standardized and efficient. Medicine could no longer be about stories of particular human bodies, since that introduces too much variability. It became about "the" human body.

Observation was not the only problem. So was language. Early scientists used different types of language to describe phenomena (e.g. narratives and sometimes the florid language of the humanities). People ascribed different meanings to the same term, gave different names to the same phenomenon, and argued over what certain terms meant or should mean. Language, too, needed to be tamed and standardized.

Scientists began to write in uniform and standardized expository prose for other professional readers within their own fields or specialties. The professional science journal article today is a prototype of standardization. It is hard to tell one article from another in terms of style, format, and methods. No "personal" voice (as there was even for Darwin) is permitted. Many papers in physics, for instance, have dozens of co-authors and no one person is responsible for the article. Such papers are as much a product of a standardized system—"big science"—as they are a product of individual scientists (Galison & Hevly 1992).

Institutions came to have great power as forces for the organization, standardization, vetting, and credentialing of scientists and other professionals. Institutions "produced" professionals and drove non-professionals, for the most part, out of business. They made language and knowledge production uniform, standardized, and, in some cases, not unlike a factory. Much the same thing was happening in workplaces, as craft workers (people who produced products in their own shops on their own schedule) were replaced by industrial workers conforming to the directives and timetable (i.e. fast) of "scientific" managers (Gee *et al.* 1996; Kanigel 1997) who claimed to use the best empirical evidence to organize work on a large scale.

Standardized, institutionalized, professional science, medicine, and workplaces have been massively successful at producing knowledge and wealth. They have allowed scientists' networks to become very large and worldwide, though quite uniform. Scientists in a given specialty all know and write for the other major producers in their area. Less than 20 percent of the people in any given specialty (a much smaller sub-area of a "discipline") produce 90 percent of the writing and research (McGrail *et al.* 2006; Shirky 2008). They include a global network and an elite "club."

Standardization of science and credentialed professionalism were creatures of both literacy and the need to control observations and interpretations of language. Literacy allowed the development of wider networks, but knowledge production stalled before there were means of standardizing observations, methods, tools, and language, as well as certifying people who were trained in standardized ways. A plethora of institutions and professional credentials arose in response. Their growth was slow and in stages, from the scientific societies and associations in Darwin's time (much like clubs where people spent a considerable amount of time demonstrating things to each other, sharing observations and arguing over what it all meant) to the massive scientific societies, professional governing bodies, and institutions of today.

Modern science and the modern industrial workplace did not need digital media to develop, but such media enhanced and enlarged both enterprises. Today robots help produce cars and gather rock samples on the moon. Machines can splice genes. Information can be stored and circulated at speeds and sizes never before possible. At a certain point, major changes in speed and size cease to be just quantitative changes and become qualitative changes, changing the very shape and nature of science and work. This is still happening today.

The creation of today's "big science" (Galison & Hevly 1992) is a major change resulting from digital media and communication tools. Big science consists of large-scale projects carried out by dozens or hundreds of scientists in different labs and institutions across the world. Big science requires degrees of organization, networking, information sharing, and expense that could only be sustained at its current levels by digital media and other technologies. The story of big science has been told before and it is not the story we want to tell here. Our point is that big science, for the most part, requires more and stronger standardized and global institutions (Galison & Hevly 1992; Price 1963; Pickering 1995).

The return of the amateur

The story we want to tell is how digital media once again allow amateurs to network with each other, outside formal institutions, to produce knowledge. We saw this happening with both theory crafting in *World of WarCraft* and with people developing and sharing knowledge about cats in the preceding two chapters.

Today, via passionate affinity spaces, forums of all kinds, blogs, Facebook, MySpace, Twitter, and many other such media, even young people can have large and global networks. If they have ideas or have designed something new, even ideas or designs that compete with professionals, they can have impact and influence. There are fan fiction writers who have thousands or millions of readers (Black 2008). There are people who design clothes, houses, and furniture for *The Sims* that have thousands or millions of users (people who download their creations) across the world (Gee & Hayes 2010).

Through digital networks and passionate affinity spaces, people can set, vet, and enforce their own standards. They can earn respect and reputation inside the passionate affinity space, based on what they do and how they interact, not based on credentials. They do not need formal institutions for support. These amateurs can, and sometimes do, challenge institutions, credentialing systems, and professionals.

Consider television ads, long the preserve of professionals working for ad agencies. Barbara Lippert, ad critic at *Adweek* magazine, has said: "The advertising industry … has to re-examine everything it has done for 100 years … Now regular people have the tools to make ads" (quoted in Collins 2005). They can readily make their ads public, as well. Companies have even begun encouraging fans to create ads for their products and these ads sometimes are better than the ads professionals make.

The professionals, of course, do not always like this competition. Furthermore, having amateurs make ads can backfire. For example, Chevrolet's marketing department decided to give a prize to the person who could create the best commercial on its web site for its then-new Tahoe SUV. The company never anticipated that many people with anti-SUV feelings would use online digital tools to create disparaging ads, ads which trashed the SUV for damaging the environment. The negative ads garnered lots of good press for their creativity and bad press for Chevrolet (Plowdell 2006).

This is typical of the new amateur experts who can compete with professionals using readily available digital tools. They are not easily controlled by institutions.

Businesses try to co-opt them, but not always with success. "The marketing community for many years has built its business model on control," says Steve Rubel, a vice president at New York public-relations firm CooperKatz, "[But] it's very hard to control the message these days" (quoted in Collins 2005).

Even after the death of amateurs as main contributors to science, there have continued to be many serious amateurs who engage in scientific inquiry. Astronomy has traditionally been the most fertile area for serious amateurs. For example, Clyde Tombaugh, an amateur, discovered Pluto in 1930 (Academy of Achievement 2010). Computers and other digital tools have greatly enhanced what amateurs can do in science and how many people can do it. For instance, Forrest Mims III, an amateur scientist, has said:

> Computers have greatly expanded the capabilities of professionals and amateurs alike, but the Internet has become the great equalizer. Several years ago I measured record low ozone over central Texas. Thanks to e-mail, I quickly notified scientists at NASA, the National Oceanic and Atmospheric Administration, and the Environmental Protection Agency and then organized a quick paper for *Eos* with them as coauthors. No one asked if I had a degree in the field; all that mattered was the significance of the event and the quality of the data. When I measured large spikes in UV radiation caused by the scattering from cumulus clouds over Hawaii's Mauna Loa Observatory, I e-mailed the results to UV specialist John Frederick. I then incorporated Frederick's comments in a communication we jointly sent to *Nature*. Frederick, the editors at *Nature*, and the peer reviewers never asked to see my credentials. Instead, they judged the work on its merits. (Mims 1999)

Amateurs' ability to use digital tools and collaborate with each other has also been harnessed for educational reform. David Williamson Shaffer, a learning scientist at the University of Wisconsin-Madison, has created an "epistemic game" devoted to urban science (Shaffer 2007). In this game, young people use a 3-D virtual world and professional urban planning tools to re-plan a part of their own town. Shaffer's virtual world is a bit like *SimCity*, but the whole experience is designed to reflect accurately how professionals engage in urban planning. The kids "role play" as urban planners.

In the game, young people have to deal with the economic, social, cultural, and environmental issues involved in urban planning. Business people in the virtual world can complain to the mayor if the planner removes parking for green space. Alternatively, "greens" can complain if the player removes green space for more parking. The player has to cope with the issues as they come up. In the end, the player writes a professional planning report and defends it, outside the game, to a real urban planner. The player is "being/doing" a professional in a way similar to what many people, old and young, are doing outside of school and formal institutions in passionate affinity spaces.

Learning languages

We live in a global world where knowing more than one language is crucial. The United States lags seriously behind other countries in the extent that its citizens master multiple languages. Being multilingual and being able to learn new languages will surely become one of the most important twenty-first century skills. Here again, young people are more deeply engaged in such learning out of school via digital media and passionate affinity spaces than they are in many schools today.

Eva Lam (2009) has written about a 16-year-old Chinese girl's IM [Instant Messaging] practices. This girl, whom Lam calls Kaiyee, participates in multiple geographically based and linguistically diverse online affinity spaces. She is developing and maintaining ties with quite different communities in which she has access to, acquires, and displays multiple linguistic resources. Kaiyee actively shapes her social networks to learn English and Cantonese, as well as to get help with math and to stay informed about the economy and job market in Shanghai.

Kaiyee immigrated to the United States of America with her parents two years prior to Lam's study. She used two IM programs (one used primarily in China) to communicate with almost 70 contacts in three networks: (a) a local network of peers from school and the local Chinese community, (b) a translocal network of friends in the USA she met through playing an online game (the English version of *MapleStory*), and (c) a transnational network of her childhood peers and relatives in China. Each network involved distinctive forms of language use, social relationships, and identity work.

In (a) the local network of Chinese immigrants, Cantonese was the primary language spoken by Kaiyee's peers. They adopted the practice of using a combination of Mandarin and Cantonese, along with the conventions of IM, to interact. For Kaiyee (a speaker of both Mandarin and her local dialect in Shanghai, but not of Cantonese), this was a way to improve her Cantonese and thus her affiliation with local immigrants.

In (b) the translocal gaming network, Kaiyee and her friends incorporated linguistic features of African American Vernacular English and lexicon related to hip-hop culture in their messages. The use of this "hybrid vernacular English" allowed Kaiyee to develop affiliations with Asian-Americans who participated in an urban-identified youth culture.

In (c), the transnational network, Kaiyee and her contacts blended Shanghainese and Mandarin within and across entries. Kaiyee perceived this network as a means of asserting and sustaining her Shanghainese identity and cultural knowledge (for example, staying informed about new Shanghainese terms), as well as maintaining affiliations with Shanghainese young people and gaining knowledge about Shanghai's economic development. A notable aspect of the use of Shanghainese orthography is that this is primarily a spoken dialect; writing in Shanghainese is actively discouraged in China, but is becoming popularized in electronic communication.

Kaiyee is crossing various linguistic, cultural, national, and identity borders. She is gaining a massive degree of meta-knowledge about how language, culture, and identity work in the global world. She has a wide, global network. She is truly a global citizen. She is using a social medium (IMing), that some consider trivial, to "school" herself for the twenty-first century.

Cultivation and shape-shifting portfolio people

Passionate affinity learning and the work of amateurs have a great many implications. It is too soon to make grand generalizations about their impact. Here we want to consider but one implication of the out-of-school learning available today. We argue that such learning is creating a new basis for social class in developed countries. Certain types of out-of-school learning allow some families to "cultivate" their children into what we later call "shape-shifting portfolio people" (Gee 2006). Such people, we argue, will be the dominant upper class in developed capitalist societies.

In a close ethnographic study of child rearing in different homes, Annette Lareau (2003), in her book *Unequal Childhoods*, identified two different models of what it means to raise children. One model she calls the "cultivation model." This model is applied mostly, though not exclusively, by middle- and upper-middle-class parents. The other model she calls the "natural growth model." This model is applied mostly, though not exclusively, by parents in the working class or poor parents.

When parents hold the cultivation model of child rearing, they treat their child like a plant that must be constantly monitored and tended. They talk a good deal to their children, especially about topics that do not just involve the here and now. They use a good deal of "book language" and adult vocabulary around their children, especially in the areas where their children have become "little experts," something these parents encourage.

Even though they are the ultimate authorities in their homes, these parents negotiate with their children so their children get plenty of practice in developing arguments and explanations. They arrange, monitor, and facilitate a great number of activities for their children, such as museum trips, travel, camps, lessons (e.g. music), and special out-of-school activities (e.g. ballet). Through these activities, they heavily structure their children's free time (and, yes, sometimes over-stress the children). They encourage their children to look adults in the eye and to present themselves to others as a confident and knowledgeable person, or at least a person with a right to an opinion. They encourage their children to develop mastery with digital tools, using things like games as a gateway, and help their child relate this mastery to literacy and knowledge development.

Cultivated children can be, in some cases, too empowered, perhaps even at times obnoxious. They can be over-stressed and need more free time to just be children or even childish. Their parents too can be overly empowered and obnoxious. Regardless of what you think of such parents and their children, the evidence is overwhelming that the cultivation model is deeply connected to success in school and to aspects of success in society, at least at the level of income and higher-status jobs. This form of child rearing and its relationship to economic success may be a bad or good thing, but it will not go away unless we radically change how our society works. In the meantime, we need to find ways to help children who get less such cultivation at home.

When parents hold the natural growth model, they treat their children like a plant that, with rich enough soil and nutrients, can be left to develop naturally. Such parents love their children and care for them deeply and well. But they do not feel the need to intervene constantly in their children's lives, from the earliest years on. Often they cannot intervene as much as more well-off parents because they are busy working and surviving. They talk less to their children and use less book-like and adult language with them. They tend to use more directives and commands with children and not negotiate with them. They expect their children to be respectful and deferential to adults. They do not structure all their children's free time and expect them to learn to find things to do with their peers and by themselves. They do not attempt to direct their children's use of digital media (like games) toward school-based skills, an interest in computer software or higher-order literacy skills.

Children raised with the natural growth model are often hard working, self-sustaining, and respectful. They are not always comfortable with putting themselves forward or presenting themselves as knowledgeable to adults, even when they are. They are not always comfortable with engaging in arguments, explanations, or sharing opinions with adults, especially those they do not know. They have not built up much language, experience, and knowledge connected to the myriad of activities children raised with the cultivation model have experienced.

Many children raised with the natural growth model have done just fine in school and have significant success in life. But if we look on a statistical level at group trends, they tend to do significantly less well in school and in society, at least in regard to income and positions of power and status, which, of course, are not the only or even the most important markers of success. We acknowledge, too, that the two models we have discussed are really poles of a continuum and there are parenting styles in-between.

Despite all the reservations and concessions we can and must make, we have here an equity crisis. It is an equity crisis that is getting bigger and increasingly involves digital tools, including video games. Children from more privileged homes, raised with the cultivation model, are acquiring a myriad of skills, values, and attitudes that contribute to success in school and to certain sorts of success in society that should be open to everyone. Much of the mentoring and learning these children are gaining is at home with their parents and in interactions with many others, peers and adults, on the Internet, as well as face-to-face in the real world. Digital media like games, along with many other digital tools, are making it easier to "cultivate" a child and are allowing children to get more mentoring, mentoring that now often goes well beyond their parents.

Many skills these children acquire are not even on offer in most of our schools, especially the schools many less-advantaged children attend. Digital media, when coupled with the cultivation model, can widen gaps in knowledge, literacy, and technological skills between rich and poor kids (Neuman & Celano 2006). The existing gaps are bad enough. We need to ask ourselves how we can cultivate all our children, in and out of school, while at the same time widening our ideas about success, beyond achievement in schools as it is currently defined, and purely monetary success later.

The new capitalism

The sort of capitalism we associate with the great economic success of the United States after World War II can be called the "old capitalism" (it is sometimes called "Fordism"). It is the capitalism of large industries and assembly lines (Gee *et al.* 1996). This old capitalism has been transformed by science, technology, and the global world. It is not gone. It still exists as a main force in the developing countries (where many of the developed world's industrial jobs have "disappeared" to) and as a background and declining force in the "developed world."

The old capitalism, like the growth of professional science, was a creature of standardization. Thanks to people like Fredrick Winslow Taylor (Kanigel 1997), work in the old capitalism came to be carried out at a pace and in terms of procedures determined by a "science" of efficiency, not by workers themselves. This "science" led to the standardization of work processes in the name of efficiency and profit.

A top-down system was created in which knowledge and control existed at the top (the bosses) and not at the bottom (the workers). Middle managers conveyed and mediated knowledge, information, and control between the top and the bottom. This became how knowledge was viewed in schools: knowledge was a system of expertise, owned by specialists, and imposed top-down on students.

In a sense Taylorism "worked." It eventually made workers "middle class" as it spread the gains of productivity to much of society. The majority of workers had unions and wages that ensured they could buy the commodities that identified people as middle class in the 1950s and 1960s.

However, by the 1970s, advances in science and technology allowed much wider global competition since modern conditions of work and the mass production of commodities could now be carried out successfully in a great variety of countries, even in some so-called "developing countries" (Greider 1997). Industrial jobs migrated to low cost centers, away from developed countries like the United States, and the power of national unions eroded.

As industrial jobs were lost, the employment structure of developed countries changed. In developed countries, the structure became something like the following: about one-fifth of the population became what Robert Reich (1992) called "symbol analysts." Symbol analysts are people who create or manage new knowledge, designs, products, and services and are paid well for it.

One-fifth of the population became what we might call "technical workers," workers who must master technical or specialized knowledge, but who are not necessarily paid nearly as well as the symbol analysts. Much of their work is routine and uses "smart tools" (e.g. machines can now splice genes and they are managed by technical workers who need not understand all the deep details of gene splicing and surely did not invent the procedures to do it).

The category of technical workers is a mixed bag. Some of these workers are stuffing electronic circuit boards using statistical information about quality and following complicated diagrams. Others are family doctors following procedures set by insurance companies and using tests performed by machines and technicians. Some conduct routine financial matters (largely controlled by computers now) in banks and other financial institutions. Many college professors (remembering that 20 percent of the people in a specialty do 90 percent of the publication) are also in this category.

Three-fifths of all workers (the vast majority) became service workers and the relatively small number of remaining industrial and manual workers. These workers are often (though not always) paid poorly with few benefits and they are often given a fair amount of responsibility. They are asked to represent the company as they deal with customers, though they are paid infinitely less than the company's CEO and managers. A large number of these workers are employed in retail stores of all sorts (e.g. Walmart), though there are many other types of service workers (e.g. workers in restaurants, health care, call centers, janitorial services, banks, and so forth) with new kinds of service work continually being invented (e.g. coaches to help young students prepare for getting into a good college, personal trainers, dog walkers, and many more to come).

In our new global capitalism, the biggest profits do not come from commodities (mass-produced products such as televisions, bikes, cars, and washing machines can be produced anywhere, so there is considerable competition that drives prices down for any standard models). Big profits come from designing new services, new products, and new knowledge for different niches, markets, and lifestyles (Greider 1997). Often people buy such services, knowledge, or products not based on price, but on status. Think of the upper-middle-class parents (before the global economic crisis that started in 2008) driving down the road in their tank-like Hummer taking their middle-school child to his or her once weekly meeting with a college counselor who helps prepare the child for admission into an elite private college. The family is not cost conscious about the Hummer, the counselor, or the college; what matters is the status associated with each.

Much work in the new capitalism involves teams and collaboration, based on the idea that in a fast changing environment, where knowledge goes out of date rapidly and technological innovation is common. A team can behave more intelligently than any individual by pooling and distributing knowledge (Gee *et al.* 1996). In the new capitalism, work is more and more *project-based*. A team comes together to carry out a project and when the project changes or is completed, the team reassembles and its members move on to other projects in the same business or others. Security in the new capitalism, such as it is, is rooted not in jobs and wages, but in what we will call one's *"portfolio."* By one's portfolio we mean the skills, achievements, and previous experiences that a person "owns" and that he or she can leverage to position him- or herself for new opportunities in changed times.

Shape-shifting portfolio people

The new capitalism in developed countries is about keeping up with fast-paced change, innovating new products and services (and "needs"), and learning new skills as old ones go out of date. People will have multiple jobs and even careers in their lifetimes. Given the pace of change, many of the jobs that they will do, and the skills they will need, will not yet exist when they leave school.

The business literature argues that this new world requires what we may call "shape-shifting portfolio people" (Gee 2000; Gee 2006; Gee & Crawford 1998; Gee *et al.* 2001). Shape-shifting portfolio people are people who see themselves in entrepreneurial terms. That is, they see themselves as free agents in charge of their own selves as if those selves were projects or businesses. They believe they must manage their own risky career trajectories through building up a variety of skills, experiences, and achievements, in terms of which they can define themselves as successful now and worthy of more success later. Their set of skills, experiences, and achievements, at any one time, constitutes their portfolio.

They must also stand ready and able to rearrange these skills, experiences, and achievements creatively (that is, to shape-shift into different identities) in order to define themselves anew (as competent and worthy) for changed circumstances. If I am now an "X," and the economy no longer needs "Xs," or "Xs" are no longer the right thing to be in society, but now "Ys" are called for, then I have to be able to shape-shift quickly into a Y.

In earlier work we have argued that well-off teens today see home, community, school, and society in just such terms (Gee 2000; Gee 2006; Gee & Crawford 1998; Gee *et al.* 2001). They seek to pick up a variety of experiences (e.g. the "right" sort of summer camps, travel, and special activities), skills (not just school-based skills, but a wide variety of interactional, aesthetic, and technological skills), and achievements (honors, awards, projects) in terms of which they can define themselves as worthy of admission to elite educational institutions and worthy of professional success later in life. They think and act, from quite early in life, in terms of their "resume." School is not the only, perhaps not even the central, site for experiences that fill up one's resume. Many skills and achievements come from young people's interactions in passionate affinity spaces and other sorts of interest-driven groups.

Social class means something different in the new capitalism than it did in the old. In the old capitalism there was a broad and massive "middle class" that was defined by one's ability to obtain and consume standardized commodities (thus, in the United States, "working-class" people had union jobs and good benefits, often owned their own homes, and had commodities like televisions, cars, and washing machines, and always referred to themselves as "middle class"; today many of these jobs are no longer unionized nor carrying good benefits). The upper-middle class and upper classes tended to own businesses, big and small, the sources of production.

In the new capitalism, one's social class is defined by the nature of one's portfolio, the sorts of intellectual, technical, and cultural experiences, skills, and achievements one has accrued (which one shares, by and large, with the "right" sort of people) and one's ability to manage these in a shape-shifting way. One's portfolio correlates with one's parents' income (though by no means perfectly), but what matters is the portfolio and the way in which it is viewed and managed. If you have no portfolio or do not view yourself in portfolio terms, then you are at risk in the new capitalism.

In today's world, in developed countries, parents "cultivate" their children via digital media, passionate affinity spaces, other interest-driven groups, and various special activities. They mentor them and encourage them to develop interests and passions and persist past failure to gain skills, many of the so-called twenty-first century skills like being tech savvy, being able to collaborate, innovate, and produce knowledge, and being able to engage in system thinking and design work.

These young people take on the identity of lifelong learners, comfortable with technical matters and with technology. They see themselves as managers of ever growing and ever re-arrangeable skills, experiences, and talents that will suit them for a fast changing, demanding, risky, and unpredictable world. They become portfolio shape-shifting people and the new "upper class" in the global world.

Mobility and citizenship

Social class and security in the global world depend on "mobility" in both literal and several figurative senses (Bauman 1998, 2000). Modern global capitalism, just like the older industrial capitalism, but at a much faster pace, transforms, often eventually destroys, localities, and then moves on (witness Detroit, much of the Gulf of Mexico, and the drought stricken Southwest in the United States). People who can move when things turn bad can leave the people who cannot or will not move to clean up the mess and live with its consequences.

Mobility is not just physical. People who have wide networks across the world, sharing information with people across the country and the world, are less dependent on local circumstances than people who do not have such networks, even if they do not physically leave. Their work may often involve interacting with people via computers and other forms of digital media. When the local factory closes, the workers lose their jobs, but the globally networked person does not, since his or her job really is not located in one place.

Today people who have mobility (can move their skills to other places when need be or whose skills are not attached to one site) are, for the most part, shape-shifting portfolio people. They often share more of their lifestyles, values, desires, and attitudes with other such people across the globe than they do with their fellow less mobile citizens in the poorer part of town. Indeed, they may feel little real "co-citizenship" with such people and may resent paying taxes to help them.

Robert Reich (1992) long ago raised the question of what, in the global world, would constitute or motivate national or local citizenship as shared responsibility for each other. Mobile shape-shifting portfolio people, while they often have a feeling of shared identity with others like themselves across the world, do not necessarily feel shared identity with the massive number of poor and desperate people in the global world. There is dire need today to re-imagine what citizenship is to mean in the global world.

12

WORDS, IMAGES, AND EXPERIENCES

Images

Over the last few years it has been popular to call attention to the importance of "multimodal texts" (Hull & Nelson 2005; Jewitt 2006; Jewitt & Kress 2003; Kress 2000, 2003; Kress & van Leeuwen 1996). Such texts combine different modalities, that is, words, images, sounds, and/or music. In this chapter we will discuss texts that combine just words and images. Such texts have proliferated over the last few decades. Japanese manga ("comic books"), video games, illustrated novels, ads, web sites, and videos, as well as other media productions, often combine words and images. Modern textbooks in science and other subjects contain more illustrations, graphs, and diagrams (as do newspapers) than they ever have before (Lemke 1998).

Multimodality is, of course, not remotely new. Early handwritten manuscripts (e.g. bibles) were often illustrated. Print gave rise to yet more illustrated books (including bibles again) and more ways to illustrate them. Music and words have long been combined in human cultures. Dance, poetry, ritual, and music were deeply connected in ancient Greece (Havelock 1976), as they were in many other cultures and are still in some cultures today.

What is new today is the proliferation of multimodality in so many different forms. Why has multimodality proliferated in this way and what does this proliferation mean and imply? The answer to these questions is rooted in some of the deepest properties of language itself.

We need to start with what an image is. The word "image" can mean two different things. Any visual markings are an image in one sense. But only some images represent something, that is, stand for something or mean something. We are interested here only in images that represent something, not just patterns of color and shape alone.

How does an image come to represent something? Consider a photograph of a bird, such as a lesser goldfinch. What does this picture represent? The answer may seem obvious, but it is not. Does it stand for the specific goldfinch in the picture? Does it stand for all lesser goldfinches in Sedona, Arizona, where the picture was taken? Does it stand for the species of lesser goldfinches? Or does it stand for birds in general?

The picture's meaning depends on the purpose it is intended to serve. In a scrapbook the picture may stand for a bird I saw on a given day. In a bird guide it may stand for the species. In an illustrated children's book it may stand for birds in general.

What does a drawing of a tree stand for? A specific tree, trees in a certain area, a species of trees, the forest in general, or nature? It all depends on the context of the drawing and what people do with it.

An image gains meaning, or represents something, first and foremost through a set of conventions, just as language does. The pictures in a bird guide represent species of birds because there are social conventions for how to read and use bird guides. A picture of trees on a map represents forestland through conventions about how to read and use such maps. A beautiful or famous person standing next to a car in an auto ad stands for the high lifestyle the car can bring consumers, through conventions on how we interpret ads.

Conventions are learned through experience. "Experience" will be the key concept in this chapter. If you have never been bird watching (or "birding") and have not interacted with birders, you will not know the conventions by which bird guides are used. If you have never used maps you do not know the conventions for how they are read and put to use in specific practices.

Conventions require experience with what the convention is about (the bird picture, maps, ads), the practices within which these things are used (birding, traveling or hiking, buying and selling), and the social groups of people who engage in these practices and follow these conventions (birders, travelers and hikers, buyers and sellers). Many people have traveled, associated with other travelers, and used maps. Fewer people have been birding, associated with birders, and can find and identify a great many species of birds. Of course, there are conventions for all sorts of things and activities like greeting people, politeness, eating in a restaurant, driving, dating, and so on through an endless list.

The conventions for how we understand and use images in modern society, such as photographs and commercials, are not understood by cultures that do not have these types of images or follow such conventions. People who have never seen a photograph actually cannot readily see what is in them. They do not know what to make of them (Chaplin 2006). Cats can most certainly see images, but most of them cannot and do not represent anything to the cat. A cat cannot see a picture of a bird as standing for a species of birds, or even one particular bird. They are not privy to the conventions, practices, and people who give such images a meaning.

An image gains meaning (represents something) because of two things: conventions (that some group developed some time in history) and experience with the practices and people who use these conventions (e.g. birding, birders, and birds). For images to represent something to someone, that someone must have had certain experiences in the world, experiences that are partly social (with other people and their practices) and partly "physical" (i.e. in and of the world).

Words

Exactly what we said about images applies to words. What gives a word like "bird" or "democracy" meaning? The answer is the same as we discussed for images: conventions and experiences (Gee 2004, 2010).

What is a word? Many people think that a word is given meaning by a definition (or a set of necessary and sufficient conditions that determine its use). Here is how one dictionary defines the word "bird": "Any of various warm-blooded, egg-laying, feathered vertebrates of the class Aves, having forelimbs modified to form wings" (*The Free Dictionary*, s.v. "Bird," accessed October 13, 2010, www.thefreedictionary. com/Bird).

Now you, dear reader, know very well what the word "bird" means, but you may not have known that birds were warm-blooded, that they are in the class "Aves," or that their forelimbs were modified (via an evolutionary process) into wings (and if you do not believe in evolution you will not like this last part of the definition). A formal definition clearly cannot be what determines the meaning of the word, or a good number of English speakers would not know what this common word means.

Here is a definition of "democracy:" "government by the people; *especially*: rule of the majority … a government in which the supreme power is vested in the people and exercised by them directly or indirectly through a system of representation usually involving periodically held free elections" (*Merriam-Webster Online*, s.v. "democracy," www.merriam-webster.com/dictionary/democracy accessed October 13, 2010). Consider that we regularly refer to ancient Athens as a "democracy" (we sometimes say that ancient Athens was the birth of democracy), yet only free males (10 percent of the population) could vote (Sinclair 1988). We regularly refer to early America as a "democracy," though the majority (women, African Americans, and many poor people who owned no land) could not vote. Surely, then, too, we do not understand the word "democracy" strictly through a definition like this one.

The meaning of a word is a set of conventions about how it can be used and used somewhat differently in different contexts. To know these conventions one must have experiences with the word, the different contexts in which it is used, and how people who follow the conventions use the word in different contexts and how they sometimes give the word new nuances of meaning in new contexts.

Each of us has had lots of experiences with a word like "bird" or "democracy." We have heard them used in different contexts, used them with other people (and seen whether they understood us or not). We have experienced birds and democracies and heard discussions and conversations and comments about them. We have seen the conventions in action as we watched people use these words and used them ourselves (with good or bad results). This *experiential base* (set of experiences) is what gives words, just like images, meaning.

Since we have all had different experiences in the world, should not words (and images) have different meanings for each of us? To a certain extent, they do. But society, culture, and social interaction ensures that we all have many similar or related experiences in terms of which we can understand words (and images) in similar enough ways to communicate. We are "normed" (guided and corrected) by our social groups and the social interactions we have with others (Gee 1992).

Specialized groups like birders have experiences with each other (and birds) that others do not have, and use the word "bird" and related words (for example, feathers are very important to bird identification, and there are many words to describe different feathers, such as coverts and alula) and images of birds in some ways that others do not. So, too, with other specialized social groups like gamers, lawyers, and street gangs. They have different experiences, conventions, and use language in somewhat different ways than do the rest of us when they are being gamers, lawyers, and street gang members.

Just as the image of fish means fish (in one of many possible ways, for example, fish as creatures or fish as food) to many, but can stand for Christ for some Christians, so, too, a word like "work" has meanings in physics that it does not have in "everyday" life; a word like "power up" means some things to gamers it does not mean to "everyday" people; and a word like "robin" (which can stand for many different birds, for example, the American robin, the European robin, or the rufous-backed robin) means some things to birders that it does not to "everyday" people ("robin," in the US, means only the red-breasted bird we see each spring). Birders have had more experience of birds called "robin" and so the word has different meanings for them than it does for non-birders.

The reason that words and images function so similarly is two-fold. First, their meanings are based on conventions. Second, they are both given meaning through the experiences people have had with others using these conventions. And, third, words are themselves much like images.

First, think of the spoken word "tree." This can be viewed as an abstract image of a tree in the sense that it stands for some aspect of trees, just as does a picture. Even regular images can be more or less abstract. A photograph of a tree can stand for trees, so can a painting, so can a line drawing, even a very simple one. The spoken word "tree" is just a very abstract and non-iconic "picture" of a tree and it can be used to refer to trees in various ways in various different contexts just as can a picture of a tree. Conventions determine that, in English, by putting the sounds "t" "r" and "ee" together we can make an abstract picture of a tree to stand for trees in different ways in different contexts of use. We are drawing with sound, in a sense.

Images are usually in some sense "iconic." In some way, sometimes in a very abstract or crude way, they look like what they represent. Words are "sound images" (Saussure 1916), representations of things, but they are not iconic, they do not look or even usually sound like what they represent. Nonetheless, they represent (re-present) in the same way images do, through conventions that connect the word to what it represents. It is as if we agreed to let an arbitrary mark (say an H) stand for trees; we would agree to treat it as a picture of a tree or to let it serve much the same purpose. In American Sign Language, signs (words) are often iconic (in an abstract way) with a loose resemblance to what they represent (Gee & Goodhart 1988).

The written word "tree" is itself a sort of image. It is an abstract picture of the sounds "t," "r," "ee" put together. We just described this as the sound image of a tree. A written word is a picture of a picture (a representation of a representation). Some writing systems skip the translation from letters to sounds and use iconic symbols (e.g. a line drawing of a tree or a circle for the sun) to stand for things like trees.

Both words and images get meaning from conventions tied to our experience with them in use in various contexts by various groups of people. In that sense, multimodal texts composed of words and images are just made up of images or representations of different degrees of abstraction. The one proviso we must add is this: human evolution has made language a special capacity for humans that has distinctive neural systems associated with it.

Experience and language at school

In the United States there is an interesting legal definition for "opportunity to learn" (Moss *et al.* 2008). Two children have the same opportunity to learn in school if they have the same textbooks and other curricular materials. This definition is based on the idea that if two English speakers have the same texts and they can read English they are dealing with the text on equal terms. Unfortunately, this is not how language actually functions. People do not understand what they read based just on the language of the text. The experiences they have had make a big difference. Two students confronted with the same text (say in science), but who had quite different experiences, will read the text in different ways.

To illustrate this point, consider the passage below:

> Your internal nano-processors keep a very detailed record of your condition, equipment, and recent history. You can access this data at any time during play by hitting F1 to get to the Inventory screen or F2 to get to the Goals/ Notes screen. Once you have accessed your information screens, you can move between the screens by clicking on the tabs at the top of the screen. You can map other information screens to hotkeys using Settings, Keyboard/ Mouse. (Ion Storm 2000: 5)

This passage is from the manual of a video game called *Deus Ex*. As one of us discovered several years ago, reading this text without having first played the game (or any games), is a boring and frustrating experience. Every word makes sense, at some level, but without experience with the game, it is difficult to make sense of the overall passage, and it is unlikely one could make use of this information. This little manual (20 small pages) had 199 bolded headings, with each heading containing language like that above, and cross-referenced to the others. The little booklet was inexplicable.

After one has played the game for some hours, even if one is not playing it well, the text then makes completely lucid sense. Why? When one tries to read the text with no experience of the game or games like it, all one can do is interpret each word through other words that help define or explicate it. This is like inserting a definition. However, after one has played for some time (acquired some experience) each word is associated with images, actions, goals, and dialogue from the game. Now each word has a lucid meaning that one can imagine in one's head, almost like a little movie. This is why young people play first and read later.

When a person has images, actions, goals, and dialogue to attach to words, they have an embodied understanding of those words. When they can only substitute other words, like definitions, in order to understand words, they have only a verbal understanding (Gee 2004).

Words vary in meaning in different contexts. When someone says, "The coffee spilled, go get a mop," we interpret "coffee" as "liquid." When someone says, "The coffee spilled, go get a broom," we interpret "coffee" as grains. When you are holding a stuffed animal, "cat" in "The cat is fluffy" means a toy. When you are looking at Fluffy the cat, "The cat is fluffy" means a real cat. "The cat broke" can mean a porcelain cat statue. We can even give novel uses to the word "cat." Imagine we are staring at two clouds, one cat shaped and one cigar shaped and I say: "The cat is fluffy, but the cigar is not."

How words vary their meanings in different contexts is another problem with the game text above. If a person has not experienced some of the words in this text in game-related contexts (e.g. "condition") or computer contexts (e.g. "tab"), then he or she cannot give the words their appropriately nuanced contextual meanings. When a person can give a word its appropriate, contextually specific meaning, we can say the person has a "situated meaning" for the word (Gee 2004, 2010).

If one person has embodied and situated meanings for a text (like the game text above) and another has not (and has, at best, verbal meanings), then they do not, in fact, have an equal opportunity to learn from the text. The person with situated and embodied meanings is going to understand the text in a deeper, more correct, and more useful way. One of the deepest equity problems in schools is that well-off children often have embodied and situated meanings for the language in their school texts, since they are more likely to have experiences related to the content of these texts, than do poorer children. For example, if a young person is confronted with a passage on monkeys in a reading test, the child who has experienced monkeys, animals, and nature in books, media, talk, and trips can often answer many of the questions without even reading the text.

Consider the excerpt below from a high school science text:

> The destruction of a land surface by the combined effects of abrasion and removal of weathered material by transporting agents is called erosion. ... The production of rock waste by mechanical processes and chemical changes is called weathering. (Martin 1990: 93)

To a geologist, or a student who has been allowed to "play the game" of geology by actually doing some, the words in this text have embodied and situated meanings, just like a gamer has for the game text above. The student who can only define the words has only verbal meanings and they are as helpful here (not much) as they were in the game text.

Our schools give students "game manuals" (a geology text) without the "game" (geology), but it is the "game" that gives embodied and situated (i.e. useful) meanings to the words in the text. Students who have embodied and situated meanings can use what they read to solve problems (i.e. play the "game"), those who have only verbal meanings often cannot. For example, in one study, college physics students who could write down Newton's laws of motion could not say how many forces are impinging on a coin thrown into the air (though this can be deduced from Newton's laws). They could, however, pass a paper and pencil test in their physics class and get a good grade. They had only a verbal understanding of Newton's laws, not an embodied and situated understanding that allowed them to apply the laws in different contexts to solve problems (Chi *et al.* 1981).

We develop embodied and situated meanings through experiences in the world of things, talk, texts, contexts, and media that provide images, actions, goals, and interactive dialogue that we can relate to words. We have lived in the world that the words of a text are about. So experience is crucial and children who have widely different experiences do not have the same opportunity to learn, regardless of legal definitions of the term.

How understanding and mastery grow

We have argued that understandings of language are lucid and useful when they are embodied and situated. These understandings are, in a sense, concrete. Someone may object to this claim: "People, especially experts, often have quite abstract understandings. How do you account for this?"

People can have abstract understandings most certainly, but they grow from concrete, embodied, and situated understandings. People start with such concrete understandings, and as they gain more related experience in an area, they gradually learn to find patterns in this experience and represent that experience more abstractly. For example, a learner who has learned, through simulations or actual experiences in a lab or the world, how Newton's laws of motion apply to one situation (e.g. an accelerating car in a race) gains an embodied and situated understanding of those laws. As they gain such understanding in more and more situations, they eventually come to see the laws as quite general and can think about them in quite abstract ways as applying to a great many situations (diSessa 2000). Their understandings are now embodied, situated, and abstract.

Experience

A question, however, arises as to why multimodality of all sorts has so proliferated in the digital age. Part of the answer lies in the notion of experience, which
we have seen is crucial for understanding both images and language. For a better
understanding of the connection between experience and words and images in the
modern world, we need to discuss the new capitalism (Gee *et al.* 1996).

In an earlier chapter, we discussed the old capitalism and the newer global
capitalism we have today. The old capitalism was about commodities (Greider
1997; Leach 1993). Commodities are products and services that become mass
produced and, thus, inexpensive enough for most people to own. Thanks to
the success of industrial capitalism (e.g. auto assembly plants, steel mills, electronic assembly plants), things like cars, radios, televisions, washing machines,
bicycles, telephones, and, to a certain extent, houses became commodities.
Working-class people had strong unions and good wages and benefits. They
could readily afford commodities and defined themselves, in the United States,
as "middle class."

Global competition eventually put an end to the old capitalism. Thanks to the
spread of science and technology by the 1970s commodities could be and were
produced in many countries. This drove down their price (and profit) further and
made such commodities more cost effective to produce with cheap labor outside
the United States and other developed countries (Greider 1997).

In developed countries profit was increasingly connected to being first on the
market with a new product or service (when it was not yet a commodity and when
a company could dominate the market). This required people with the creativity
to invent such new products and services and to see or create the need for them
(Drucker 1993; Kelly 1994; Thurow 1999). People who designed and invented
things, people who produced new knowledge, came to be rewarded more and more
compared to others who simply provided or sold these products and services to
others once they were invented.

Profit came to depend less on mass markets for standardized products and services (commodities) and more on creating new markets and new niches within
markets. Companies began to market and sell their products and services in terms
of different lifestyles, identities, and values (Seabrook 2000). If I convince you that
your health-conscious, green, but yuppie lifestyle and identity means you should
buy a certain sort of car that "fits" with that identity, I have segmented the market.
I can sell different types of cars to different types of people. Cars today are relatively
cheap to produce in terms of materials in them and the labor required to make
them. However, different sorts of people will buy different models, thinking they
are buying meaningfully different things, because the cars are designed differently
to speak to different lifestyles and identities.

In many cases, as people associate what they consume with different identities,
lifestyles, and values they share with others "like them," they become less sensitive
to cost. They will pay more for a cup of coffee that says "who" they are (e.g. at

Starbucks rather than at McDonald's), regardless of the fact that the coffee is over-priced and costs about the same to produce as any other coffee.

Advertisers not only customize their ads in terms of different lifestyle identities and values. They also create these identities and values (Rifkin 2000). For example, they may instill a desire among women to see themselves as "modern" and "with it" in ways (e.g. by smoking a certain brand of cigarette, driving a certain type of car, or wearing a certain sort of bathing suit) that are more a product of the ad firm than of women themselves. If the women adopt these values and identities they become "real" and connected to "needs" for certain products and services.

People have different lifestyles and identities based on different life experiences with others whom they see as "like them": for example, modern urban Latino; professional, but stay-at-home mom; social media fanatic; young professional urban pioneer; edge-city suburbanite; third-generation African American college woman; upper-class "anti-government" libertarian. Since companies want to create new markets, they now often market or try to create such niche identities (Frank 2000; Rifkin 2000; Seabrook 2000).

When we discussed shape-shifting portfolio people in Chapter 11, we argued that people who seek success in developed countries often "sell" themselves as portfolios of ever-rearrangeable skills that they have attained through their experiences in school and increasingly out of school in passionate affinity spaces and other interest-driven groups and activities. They seek new skills to enlarge their portfolios and create ever more shifting identities to meet ever-new opportunities or crises.

We live now in a world where new identities and market niches, based on newly created or newly defined experiences (e.g. adventure travel, living green, using social media, living in the "right" neighborhood or going to the "right" college) are crucial and defining. Experience is the basis for understanding and creating new ways with words and images and, thus, too, multimodal texts. Thus, it is not surprising that, in a world where innovation, creativity, design, and the creation of new experiences are crucial for economic success, multimodal texts have proliferated. They can allow for more aspects of experience to be represented and juxtaposed efficiently and creatively than can texts composed merely of words. They can also allow us to lie and manipulate in more creative ways, as well. What we are looking at, in reality, is the proliferation of representations of all sorts—re-presentations of ever more aspects of ever more realities, virtual and "real."

It is hard to describe how to tie a shoe. Our experience of tying shoes is so tacit and complexly tied to the body that it is difficult to put into words. Pictures of the stages of shoe tying, with some verbal annotations, would be much more useful. This is why more and more scientific and technical books juxtapose words and images, since they seek to explicate things and processes that are so complex and intricate that words and images are more efficient than words or images alone. New technologies have allowed scientists to see more and to experience more than any humans ever have (e.g. chromosomes and galaxies, molecules and cells). It is not surprising for this reason, too, that both new words and new images, and multimodal texts, have proliferated.

On the other hand, consider the quote below from Consumers International about Toyota ads:

> Another advertisement, this time from New Zealand, states that the RAV4 Diesel is "the car nature wants to own" and shows rabbits climbing into the driver's seat ... With CO_2 emission of over 170 g/km, we're not so sure.
>
> Yet any claims, accurate or not, that Toyota makes about the minimal environmental impact of its vehicles are put into perspective by one of the company's flagship marketing exercises.
>
> Promoted globally in 2007 and 2008, including a TV series tie-in, Toyota's Hilux Arctic Challenge involved driving a Hilux SUV to the North Pole. It was hailed as the first vehicle ever to do so. Considering the speed at which the Arctic ice sheets are melting due to climate change, it may also be the last. (Consumers International 2008)

An ad that has rabbits trying to get into a car to drive it and says "The car nature wants to own" is using images and words to say what in words alone would sound silly, but in images and words can be dismissed as funny. The ad is a lie, of course. However, saying in words: "This is a car nature wants to own even though its CO_2 emissions contribute to environmental destruction" would make the lie readily apparent.

As multimodal texts like the ad we discussed above proliferate, we all need more experiences that allow us to be critical. We have to become critical consumers of multimodal texts and to take the example of the ad, it helps to have experienced environmental damage, debates about global warming, and manipulative ads.

Is all this good or bad? It is far too complex to be simply one or the other. This situation is a complex mixture of possibilities and perils. Such a world certainly requires that people can "read" words, images, and multimodal texts critically in terms of asking whose interests are served and whose are not, and what the agendas were of the producers of those words, images, and texts. This criticality requires yet more experience, though perhaps experiences of a different sort from those of non-critical consumers. One must have experienced the world in terms of ethical considerations about equity, fairness, and a just and humane civil society, for example, by actually comporting with people who have suffered injustice and inequality, or actually seeing how institutions like schools can function to sort people unfairly based on their homes and social class and not their real intelligence. These experiences are in shorter supply than other experiences (e.g. eating at the newest trendy restaurant in town) that lead people simply to aspire to "co-consume" with their fellow lifestyle and social class "mates."

13

THREE SOCIAL FORMATIONS

Interpretation and context

Language unites us and separates us. We understand each other because we speak the same language. Yet language can give rise to conflict even when people speak the same language. Language is always interpreted relative to specific contexts of use (Gee 2010). This is where troubles can arise.

What is "context"? In face-to-face communication, context includes the physical setting in which the communication takes place and everything in this setting; the bodies, eye gaze, gestures, and movements of those present; what has previously been said and done by those involved in the communication; and any shared knowledge those involved have, including shared cultural knowledge.

As an example, consider how you know what the word "work" means in the following sentences:

1 I am at work now.
2 Relationships shouldn't take work.
3 That is a real work of art.
4 Work is changing in the twenty-first century.
5 That idea won't work.

You know what "work" means in each case because you can, based on your cultural knowledge and experiences in the world, including conversations with others, imagine contexts in which the word has specific, though different meanings. In (1) the word means a particular job; in (2) it means effort one does not enjoy; in (3) it means something like an achievement; in (4) it means the whole world of jobs and professions; and in (5) it means that the idea is not correct or helpful. A word can have different meanings in the same sentence: "Your work shouldn't be work" means "Your job shouldn't consist of effort you don't enjoy."

If we disagree about context (about what should be taken as shared knowledge, for instance), we can disagree over what language means in use. Your "freedom fighter" might be my "terrorist" depending on how we see certain causes and conflicts. If someone says, "It's unbelievable he wants to be a priest," the person may be assuming that the listener shares a view that becoming a priest is undesirable, for any of several reasons. If the listener does not, he or she will be taken aback, confused, or bothered by the comment.

Oral cultures, literate cultures, and today's digital cultures have different problems with interpretation and context. These problems lead to different means of controlling language and its interpretations. We now turn to these issues, looking at three "social formations": one "oral," one "literate," and one "digital."

The oral social formation

As we discussed in an earlier chapter, in an oral culture (a culture with no or very limited literacy), when a person makes a claim and there are problems of interpretation (either about what is meant or whether what was said was true or not) listeners can question the speaker. Speakers and listeners can negotiate meaning. Interpretation can be dialogic, interactive, and relatively flexible. Of course, powerful people (as Socrates found out) do not always like being asked what they mean or why they claim what they claim.

On the other hand, imagine that a person in an oral culture makes an important claim about the culture's past. How do people know the person is correct or telling the truth? There are no records. For claims that are important to the culture, say about ancestors, the origins of the group, or religious beliefs, how can a claim be supported and how can questions about meaning or truth be answered or stopped? Since there are no records, often the only way to establish a claim and stop questions is authority, authority based on force, age, or status. While oral cultures certainly appeal to evidence in many situations, evidence for many highly consequential claims is limited without literacy.

This system, in which interactive, dialogic, flexible interpretation was controlled by authority, lasted long past the introduction of literacy. Literacy did not kill it quickly or completely. Today many religions and churches still use top-down, coercive authority (e.g. the threat of Hell) to control interpretations of written scripture. For centuries even claims about the human body and the world rested less on evidence than on authority (Brown 1988; Laqueur 1990). What the "ancients" (e.g. Galen and Aristotle) said or the Church dictated trumped evidence (as Galileo found out). Eventually, however, literacy, especially with the introduction of print, led to a different system for establishing meaning and validating interpretations.

The literate social formation

The introduction of literacy led to records of the past and records of people's observations and experiences in the world. Many more claims and types of claims can be checked. When an authority makes a claim, people can now produce evidence that it is not true or that what is claimed to be fact is actually fiction or metaphor. Of course, authorities often do not react well to this challenge to their status and power.

Starting with the Renaissance and the Enlightenment, eventually, for many claims, evidence came to trump authority. Claims were not true because elders, elites, leaders, or priests said them, but because there was evidence to support them. This ability to make records gave birth to true science, which is an empirical enterprise. It also called into question the basis of much authority in state and church and helped give rise (fitfully and incompletely) to democracy, meritocracy, and belief in the equality of human beings.

A literate culture (a culture where literacy is pervasive) has a new problem with interpretation, however. As we discussed previously, written texts can travel across time and space. The text is often interpreted at a different time and place (in a different context) than when it was first produced. This is a problem for interpreting the Bible and Shakespeare, for instance, and many other texts that we use today but were written very long ago.

An additional problem with literacy is that written texts seem, even in their original context of production, to be "decontextualized." Unlike face-to-face communication where what is meant often depends a good deal on context (what people can see and share, including gestures and facial expressions), written texts sometimes seem to "put everything into words." They appear to be "explicit" in ways that face-to-face communication is not.

In reality no written texts are decontextualized (Gee 2008a). No written text can say everything explicitly in words. Any text must assume that readers share some knowledge with the writer that allows them to make obvious inferences and otherwise "fill in the gaps" in a particular description or argument. Shakespeare's work assumes that readers shared many cultural and religious beliefs, as well as lots of everyday knowledge, that readers today do not. Shakespeare never dreamed that so much of what he thought "everyone" knew and took for granted would in the future be obsolete. This is why he is hard to read today, even though his plays were a form of popular entertainment in their own time.

What is true, and problematic, is not that written texts are decontextualized, but that they are "fixed" and inflexible in ways that speech is not. In face-to-face conversation and even in storytelling, listeners can interrupt and ask speakers what they really mean and why they are saying what they are. Speech, as we said above, is dialogic and interactive. Interpretation can be negotiated and changed. The speaker can clarify and agree on meanings with his or her listeners.

Writing is not dialogic and interactive in the same way as speech is. Readers cannot directly interrogate the author and they cannot negotiate with the author. They can do these things in their heads, but in that case they are having a mental dialogue between themselves and their image of who the author is. Readers often cannot check or, at least, do not know what authors thought the relevant context was for their work, what knowledge, assumptions, experiences, and values they assumed were shared by themselves and their readers.

For example, when Shakespeare wrote his famous lines "Golden lads and girls all must/As chimney sweepers come to dust" (from the funeral song of Act IV, Scene 2 of *Cymbeline*) he assumed that people knew that the term "chimney sweepers" could stand for chimney sweeps (people who sweep chimneys) or the brush they use to do the job, a brush that resembles a dandelion when it has gone to seed. In Shakespeare's time "golden lads" and "chimney sweepers" were colloquialisms for the various stages of the dandelion, which starts as a yellow flower, turns grey when it has gone to seed, and then blows off in the wind as dust (Knapp 2003). Most people today know none of this and so must interpret the lines in whatever context they can imagine. Today's references to film (for cameras) and records (to play music) will soon be opaque to readers, going out of date much faster than did Shakespeare's chimney sweepers.

There is an advantage to this fixedness of written texts, their lack of dialogue and negotiation. People can write texts like constitutions, religious texts, policies, and laws and spread them wide and far. The belief that texts are explicit means that they can be used to fix or standardize rules, laws, and policies across a large space.

However, written texts are actually open to different contextually sensitive interpretations and may be used long after they were first written. Thus, institutions arise to provide "official" interpretations, removed from the contextually specific negotiations of face-to-face communication. These are institutions like courts, legislative bodies, expert commissions, institutions and societies set up to control standards and measurements (e.g. for time, length, and quantitative properties for all sorts of things like bridges and roads). Such institutions often claim the texts they regulate are fixed and "decontextualized," when, in reality, they are not.

This sort of top-down control over the interpretation of written laws, standards, procedures, policies, and important documents requires institutions. Once again we see the ties between literacy and formal institutions. The two together allowed large states and large enterprises (like industries and big science) to flourish. Interpretation, standards, values, and procedures could be set, standardized, and enforced across large and dispersed territories, from the top down.

This system of relatively fixed interpretations controlled by institutions gives rise to two important classes of actors: bureaucrats and technical experts or specialists. Bureaucrats and technical experts specialize in the interpretation of documents in given areas (e.g. law, commerce, medicine, sports, and so forth). Their word replaces the coercive authority of oral cultures (Hacking 1990; Steinberger 2005). Their authority is based on their special knowledge and the credentials (degrees) they have earned that "certify" that knowledge. They claim to make their decision based on facts (evidence), not power or self-interest, but it can be hard at times to know when they are acting on their own behalf, or in the interest of people in power, and when they are really being "objective," as they claim.

Today we read the Bible and Shakespeare even when we know or care little about the contexts in which they were originally produced. We believe they have universal meanings; indeed, that is why we consider them "canonical." But when texts are taken out of their contexts of production, they become open to many more interpretations, since we can ignore constraints on interpretation that would have been established by their original context. The problem becomes how to stop this proliferation of interpretation. To do so, we rely on experts (priests and literary critics) supported by institutions (churches and universities) who claim to really know what the texts mean, either because they know a great deal about their original contexts of production or, more commonly, because they have a special ability to discern their "real" and "deep" meanings apart from such contexts. The experts can even claim that there are "deep secrets" in such texts that only they, and people who have been initiated by them, know (Kermode 1979).

In an oral culture, interpretation is (potentially) interactive, dialogic, flexible, but controlled in consequential cases by authority (force or status, not evidence). In modern literate societies, interpretation is relatively fixed and less interactive, dialogic, and flexible, but the fixed interpretations are "adjusted" by institutions and their bureaucrats and experts (since no interpretations are truly fixed or without a need for dialogue, negotiation, and interaction). People, of course, do engage in interaction, dialogue, and flexible negotiation in modern literate cultures, but these dialogic interactions always are subject to the power of institutions to set standards of knowledge, procedure, and truth based on their control of written texts.

The digital social formation

The oral social formation consisted of interactive, flexible, dialogic interpretation controlled in consequential cases by authority. The literate formation was comprised of relatively fixed and standardized interpretations controlled by institutions. The oral formation lasted long into the beginnings of literacy in society. The literate formation is still very much alive. Nonetheless, the place of the literate formation in society is and will change as a digital social formation grows in power.

Digital media allow people to use written language in ways that resemble how people use face-to-face oral language. People can communicate at great distances in real time through the Internet and various sorts of social media. When people post a text online, send a text message, or use Twitter, readers can quickly get into dialogue with them and ask them, as in an oral culture, what they mean, why they mean it, and why they think it is true. There is often no authority with real power like the kings, priests, and dictators of old or the formal institutions of the literate formation to interpret or restrict what is said. Some countries try to control such digital talk, but they are successful only to a limited extent.

Digital media bring flexible, dialogic, interactive interpretation to written language in a quite widespread and pervasive way. In the literate social formation, institutions play a leading role in fixing, adjusting, and standardizing interpretations and norms and settling disputes top-down. Though the Internet and social media typically rely on written language, institutions are, at least so far, less powerful and have a much harder time fixing interpretations and practices top-down, though, of course, they try (see Shirky 2008, 2010; Wasik 2009 for many examples). Leetspeak (an alternative alphabet for English used primarily on the Internet) flourishes and blogs of all sorts interpret away with little control from mainstream media or the government.

Even on sites like Facebook and in games like *World of WarCraft*, both owned by for-profit companies, consumers are able regularly to talk back to the businesses and reshape their policies. Many Internet sites and interactions are set up and managed by the people who engage in them. They control interpretations and negotiate meanings for themselves. For example, on sites where people design houses, furniture, clothes, and landscapes for *The Sims* (a family and community simulation), people of all ages (12–70) and all degrees of expertise mentor each other to learn and engage in design. The participants on each site agree on norms and standards of behavior—and these differ significantly across such sites—and often negotiate and change them.

Control in the digital world is much less top-down and interactively negotiated than in the literate social formation. In the digital formation we see flexible, interactive, and dialogic interpretation often controlled neither by authority nor institutions. It is controlled, or rather shaped (control implies too much power), in many cases, through social interactions and negotiations among participants themselves.

In the digital formation even written texts dear to the literate formation, texts like Shakespeare, the Bible, or the US Constitution, become open to flexible, interactive, and dialogic interpretation as "everyday people" interact with others, and even, at times, experts, to debate interpretations (see, for example, Chapter 10 on cats). Many more people can gain access to information about the contexts in which these texts were produced and how these contexts throw into doubt some interpretations and claims. It becomes clear that the interpretation of written texts is not really as fixed as institutions (including schools) have claimed.

In a sense, the digital social formation is a return to "orality" without the power of coercive authority to control it. Coercive authority in oral cultures kept the culture together and prevented it from fragmenting into contesting interpretive groups. That is a core purpose of a king or pope. The same is true today in some countries with dictators or powerful leaders and in many religions and churches.

Institutions set standards and norms that allow for effective large-scale action and cooperation among different countries, communities, cultures, and institutions. Institutions tie a large and diverse country like the United States together. They can protect minorities from majorities in democracies.

It is important to ask, though there is yet no answer, what will cause group cohesion and large-scale cooperation when the digital social formation is operative. This formation lends itself to many fragmented "discourse communities" or passionate affinity spaces setting their own norms and enforcing their own rules and values.

Difference and commonality

What makes people feel like they are the same as other people? Early in human history, when humans were hunters and gatherers, or later when they lived in small and culturally uniform settlements, cultures were small. Everyone in the group shared the same language and had much the same knowledge of the world.

The famous anthropologist Claude Lévi-Strauss (1992; see also Lévi-Strauss 1975) once argued, in a controversial paper, that the ideal condition for humans was when groups were relatively small, quite different from each other, and lived just far enough away from each other that they did not engage in warfare, but not so far away that they could not borrow ideas from each other once in a while. Borrowed ideas became a source of change in cultures that were relatively static. Each group, over time, discovered different, but important, ways to be "human."

Lévi-Strauss felt that, thanks to modern media and technology, the world was homogenizing. Most nations, especially developed ones, were becoming more and more alike. This process has gone much further since Lévi-Strauss made his claims (in 1971 when he was invited by UNESCO to inaugurate the International Year for Action to Combat Racism). Many countries and regions are losing some of their distinctiveness as the same businesses, fashions, technologies, media, and trends spread across the globe.

When groups stayed far enough away to avoid conflict and close enough to occasionally borrow, each group represented a distinctive way to be human that was occasionally refreshed and transformed by borrowing. While each group thought they were the best or the "real" humans, as long as they stayed far enough away not to compete for resources, they often avoided conflict.

Lévi-Strauss's paper was controversial because it seemed to stress difference and distinctiveness over common humanity. Many have hoped that, in our global world, people would come to see themselves as sharing a common humanity despite national, ethnic, cultural, and linguistic differences. But as the world becomes "smaller," due to media and technology, Lévi-Strauss was correct in asserting that differences and distinctions across societies can begin to disappear or mitigate. American commercial culture, for example, has done more to "colonize" large parts of the world than overt force ever did in the heyday of colonial empires.

Co-citizenship

Any country faces the problem of how to make strangers feel like they have responsibilities to each other as fellow citizens. Humans, like many other animals, have a hard time accepting strangers and people who are not their kin. This is one reason why nations have often spread the idea (usually a myth) that everyone in the nation shares some "blood" or some deep commonality (Anderson 2006). In history, it has been far too easy for demagogues and tyrants to convince their people that those who did not share their language, color, or culture were somehow sub-human.

While humans often fear or look down on strangers and people who are different, we do, at some level, view all other humans as "like us." It is hard, for example, for most human beings to harm or kill another human when looking that other person in the face. That is why demagogues and tyrants work so hard to dehumanize the "other" and convince their followers that others are sub-human.

Unfortunately, humans are less viscerally adverse to hurting or killing other people when they cannot see them. Pilots, who as individual humans would have great trouble killing another human being face-to-face, find it much easier to bomb villages when all they can see is a mark on a screen and all they have to do is push a button at the right time. We are all aware that we feel more compassion for a starving child we see in person than the thousands of starving children in Africa we only read about in the news.

Konrad Lorenz, one of the Nobel Prize winning founders of modern ethology, argued that in the modern global world it would become crucial that humans learn, against our natures, to empathize with others even when we could not literally see them (Lorenz 2002). Only in this way could modern warfare, where killing often happens at a great distance, be mitigated. Only in this way could people see starving children across the world as worthy of attention. And yet, ironically and sadly, Lorenz's published writings during the Nazi period included support for Nazi ideas of racial purity (Eisenberg 2005).

Modern technology has done more than homogenize aspects of the global world. It has changed how people develop feelings of "co-citizenship." For centuries, people felt co-citizenship with other people in their same "nation," sometimes because of "fictions" that everyone in the nation shared something that made them the "same." However, today, in many nations, and most certainly the United States, many people feel less "co-citizenship" with others in their own country who are, say, poorer or less educated than themselves, than they do with others across the country and globe with whom they share professions, education, values, or lifestyles (Reich 1992).

Modern media and transportation have allowed some of us to communicate with many others who are far distant (and economically consume the same things we do). These people come to seem more like us than people in our own country with whom we do not share values or lifestyles. We wonder why we have the responsibility to pay taxes, say, for others in our country whom we do not see as really the "same" as us. The idea that we owe something to others because we share citizenship in a nation with them begins to weaken.

Mobility in the modern world has created a divide between people who have the resources to go it alone (for example, by paying for services) and those who do not. In less mobile days, people who needed help could call on an extended family that lived nearby. Modern economies have required people to be more mobile (Bauman 1998, 2000). People often have to move away from their original homes to obtain jobs and economic opportunities, since some areas decay and others prosper when businesses seek the lowest production costs in a globally competitive world. Many people no longer have an extended family nearby to help them when they are in need. Their family and friendship networks of reciprocity, in which people give help and get help from each other, are torn apart.

Successful professionals in the modern world typically can use their own resources to help themselves when they have problems by paying for such help. People with fewer resources must seek help from the government (whose social welfare programs are disappearing or weakening) or churches (hence the growth of fundamentalist churches that claim to be a "family" and to nourish families torn apart by the modern world). The people who have the resources to go it alone, who can move from place to place without the need for social supports, become a new global class skeptical of government and about what they owe, beyond charity, to someone else just because they happen to live in the same country.

The breakdown of the public sphere

The breakdown in feeling co-citizenship with others in our nation is connected to a much longer historical trend in Western society. Who do you think is the "real you"? Is it your private self at home with your family? Or is it your public self, out in the world at work or dealing with society at large?

Over several hundred years people in Western societies have tended to shift from a view that their public self (their public role) is their "real," "authentic," or "best" self to viewing their private self as the "real" and "authentic" one (Sennett 1977). We now feel that we are "acting," "putting on airs," "faking it," or "having to play the game" in public. We can only be "ourselves" in private with others who "accept us as we are." We consider the persona we present in public to be a façade.

This valorization of the private self has led to a deterioration of public space and the public sphere (the areas in life where we feel we share something with everyone else in our society). People, or at least some classes of people, avoid public spaces where they will encounter others who are different than them. We are familiar, for example, with wealthy people who move from their guarded-gate community to their high-style workplace, passing through poor or more urban areas on their way, areas with which they feel no attachment and for which they feel no responsibility.

In some ways, people who avoid the larger public have become more "local" as they have become more "global." They network, communicate, and engage in work with others like themselves across the world, but they inhabit increasingly more restricted spaces within their own communities and country, such as their guarded-gate community and their work enclaves.

The public sphere also has eroded through the way that modern media and technology have allowed for ever-greater proliferation of market niches that have increasingly replaced mass markets. Today, technology allows products and services to be produced efficiently on a large scale, but customized to different consumer identities, values, lifestyles, and niches. Technology has also allowed a myriad of interest and passion-driven groups to organize on the Internet and in the real world, around almost any interest or passion you can name. Though these groups can contain quite diverse kinds of people, and people can conceal their real identities, race, class, and gender, the identity they share is their common interest or passion and its concomitant values.

This raises the issue of what constitutes the "public sphere" today, that is, the place where people come together across class, racial, and ethnic differences. The public sphere in the past was defined most often as a country and its public places and institutions. We have seen, however, that today many people do not see the "public sphere" as the place where they are most "real" or "at home." They do not see the other people who constitute the "public" as like them in important ways, even as "co-citizens." At the same time, many privileged people today engage in public activities and spaces across the world with others whom they see in lifestyle, profession, wealth, interests, or values as like themselves.

Digital media and a new public sphere

Some people have argued that digital media are giving rise to a new and reinvigorated public sphere (Steinkuehler & Williams 2006). In a massively multiplayer game like *World of WarCraft* or a popular virtual world like *Second Life*, people come together from across a country and across the world, people of different social classes, values, and lifestyles. A middle-class person who never sees working-class people in the "real world" will certainly interact with them in *World of WarCraft*.

In such virtual worlds people often adopt "fictional" identities. They use avatars that they name and design as they wish. They can talk, act, and interact in very different ways than they do in their "real lives." They can play with new identities. They can refuse to share with others that they are a woman or an African American, or they can choose to share this information and use it how they wish.

Ironically, there are now many people who feel that in such virtual worlds they are finding their "real selves," who they "really are" or want to be. They sometimes form relationships, even "marriages," to other people's avatars that they value as much or more than their real world relationships and marriages. For some people, the historic escape from the public sphere to private life has now meant an escape to a virtual public sphere.

Are spaces like *World of WarCraft* and *Second Life* really new public spheres? These spaces do offer people the opportunity to interact with a massive variety of different sorts of people, including people in their own countries whom they would never associate with in real life. But at the same time, people within these virtual worlds can and do form guilds and other sorts of groups to affiliate with people like themselves, with similar values, for instance, and to exclude others. For example, *World of WarCraft* guilds have been formed for academic researchers, parents, "casual" players, women, Christians, adults only, and so forth.

Throughout the Internet and not just in virtual worlds, more and more people are joining groups with shared interests and passions, as we have discussed. These groups often agree to behave in certain ways that ensure yet more uniformity. Of course, interests and passions that people pursue on the Internet are not uncorrelated with social classes, genders, and lifestyles in the real world.

So are modern digital media giving rise to new global publics or to new forms of balkanization? It is quite possible that we are returning to a new form of Lévi-Strauss's "ideal world." We are gaining a great many interest- and passion-defined communities separate enough to stay distinctive and in just enough contact with others to borrow and steal ideas. The upside may be a mitigation of homogenization. The downside may be an even more splintered view of who is a "real" or valuable human being or one worth paying attention to and helping.

14

MULTITASKING, DIVERSITY, AND COMMONALITY

The loss of density

In our digital age there are many who claim that core skills associated with the literacy social formation are disappearing. Despite fears to the contrary, reading and writing are not dying. Most of digital media require reading and writing. Young people today often read a great deal in connection with the Internet and with digital activities like video games. Gamers write long strategy guides and share them with others (see, for example, www.gamefaqs.com). *World of WarCraft* players engage in highly technical reading and writing as they engage in theory crafting (see Chapter 9). Many young people write fan fiction based on books, movies, television shows, and games (Black 2008). The passionate affinity spaces we discussed in Chapter 7 often involve a good deal of reading and writing of different sorts (Lam 2009).

Parents and educators have complained that the "slang" and grammatical short-cuts in text messaging are harming young people's literacy skills. But recent research has shown no evidence of this. In one study, the more "textisms" students used, the higher they tended to score on measures of word-based learning and vocabulary (Whitley 2009). This really should not be surprising. Acquiring new ways with words, something people do all the time, can increase rather than decrease people's language skills. They just have a bigger repertoire. A summary of this study states:

> A factor behind the results might simply be the increased exposure to the printed word that text-messaging inspires. The fun and ease of the medium encourages extra language practice, especially by children whose skills are poor and who are otherwise discouraged from reading. (Whitley 2009)

The types of reading and writing young people do are changing. They engage in more technical reading and writing connected to their digital activities (Lenhardt &

Madden 2005). They do not read texts like novels quietly alone in their bedrooms as much, perhaps, as their parents did. Young people's reading and writing is often tied to social activities and interest-driven groups.

The most common complaint about the digital generation is that young people today cannot focus their attention for extended periods of time (Bauerline 2008; Carr 2010). They don't, it is claimed, read long texts deeply and reflectively. Canonical works like Shakespeare and Henry James are being abandoned in a world with no time for such "slow" tasks.

The playwright Richard Foreman has talked about "the replacement of complex inner density with a new kind of self-evolving under the pressure of information overload and the technology of the instantly available" (quoted in Brockman 2010: 17). He asks whether "we are becoming Pancake People—spread wide and thin as we connect with the vast network of information accessed by the mere touch of a button."

Certainly the ecology of reading and writing is changing. But it is not clear how many people read canonical works carefully, methodically, and reflectively once they became school subjects. Furthermore, while many people claim such reading gave them deep insights, sometimes these insights were the ones literary experts in university English departments demanded and which changed when theories of literary criticism changed.

We do not deny that some literary works offer deep truths about the human condition, though we doubt that these truths are best discovered as part of a curriculum intended to grade and sort people at school. We believe that great literary works need to be both part of a healthy reading diet and liberated from schools. It may be possible to use digital media to get many more people than ever involved with art and literature.

All technological changes in how we communicate, whether writing, print, or digital media, involve genuine losses. Walter Ong, a Jesuit priest and a revered scholar in the humanities, wrote eloquently about the losses suffered in the transition from oral culture to literate culture:

> Oral cultures indeed produce powerful and beautiful verbal performances of high artistic and human worth, which are no longer even possible once writing has taken possession of the psyche. Nevertheless, without writing, human consciousness cannot achieve its fuller potentials, cannot produce other beautiful and powerful creations. In this sense, orality needs to produce and is destined to produce writing. … There is hardly an oral culture or a predominantly oral culture left in the world today that is not somehow aware of the vast complex of powers forever inaccessible without literacy. This awareness is agony for persons rooted in primary orality, who want literacy passionately but who also know very well that moving into the exciting world of literacy means leaving behind much that is exciting and deeply loved in the earlier oral world. We have to die to continue living. (Ong 1982: 14–15)

The values and practices of oral cultures took a very long time to weaken or die after the introduction of literacy. We are only at the beginning of the digital age and it will take a long time for literate values and practices as we know them to transform as fully as they inevitably will. There will be gains and losses, for sure.

The historian of science George Dyson (quoted in Brockman 2010: 17) has used an analogy to Native American boatbuilding to make an important point about how the Internet and digital media are changing human thinking. He points out that in the North Pacific Ocean there were two different approaches to building a boat. The Aleuts, who lived on treeless islands, built kayaks by piecing together skeletal frameworks for their boats from fragments of wood found washed up on the beach. The Tlingit built dugout canoes by selecting entire trees out of the rainforest and removing the wood until there was nothing left but a canoe.

Dyson argues that the flood of information from the Internet has produced a similar split. When information was rare and hard to come by, produced mainly by experts and their institutions, we operated like kayak builders, collecting all available relevant fragments of information we could get our hands on to assemble the framework for our knowledge production. Now, when information is pervasive, cheap, and easy to obtain—and produced by a wide array of people—we have to learn, Dyson says, to "become dugout canoe builders, discarding unnecessary information to reveal the shape of knowledge hidden within" (Brockman 2010: 17).

Who is to say that assembling rare and hard to obtain fragments into a beautiful whole is better or worse than chipping away from a surplus until we uncover a beautiful whole? Great novelists have operated in the former way and many a great sculptor, chipping away at a block of marble, has operated in the second way. Both ways, in some fashion, will survive, but the latter may become predominant in the digital age.

In any case, we do not believe that the real issue that incites critics is the loss of slow and reflective reading. The real issue that bothers critics is the way in which many young people today multitask. This means, to the critics, that young people are not paying focused attention to anything, not just canonical literary works. They, for instance, are not paying single-minded attention to their college lectures or to newscasts either.

Multitasking

We all know that many young people today multitask in the sense that they may be searching for web sites while text messaging; playing a video game while keeping up with friends on Facebook; or watching television while doing homework on their computer in one window and keeping up with a favored web site on another.

Clifford Nass (2010), a leading media researcher and a critic of multitasking, argues that multitasking is much more ubiquitous and involves many more tasks that we commonly think. Based on surveys Nass has done at Stanford University, the average university student is "regularly using four different media streams; fewer than 5 percent of students report that they regularly use a single stream, and more than 20 percent are using six or more streams at one time" (Nass 2010: 11).

Nass argues that heavy multitaskers are "much worse than previous generations of readers at three tasks … filtering the relevant from the irrelevant, managing short-term memory, and switching from one task to another" (Nass 2010: 12). Nass's research, however, involves laboratory tasks like being asked to pay attention to red rectangles on a computer screen and ignore blue rectangles. Such tasks are not, of course, much like what people do outside of laboratories, where what they pay attention to, however divided their attention, is more meaningful than shapes on a screen.

Nass and other critics are really claiming, at heart, that when people do multiple tasks at once they perform less well on any one of them than had they performed just that one. Dividing attention is not as effective as focusing it on one thing at a time.

Human short-term memory and attentional capacity are limited. All things being equal, it is clear that anyone can do one thing better than many in the same time period. But this is really not the point. The point is: how do people do what they need to do, as best as they can, in the time they have?

We have watched a teenage boy play video games on an Xbox with his laptop open to keep abreast of his friends on Facebook. Could he have done either one task better alone? Probably. But he finishes his games in record time compared to other gamers and there are no complaints from his Facebook friends. He has clearly managed to do two things well in an impressively short time for what he accomplished. Furthermore, he enjoys both activities more by doing them together. For him, they may really be one "mixed" activity.

Long before the digital age, humans had to be multitaskers. As our discussion has revealed throughout this book, face-to-face oral communication, the primordial form of communication for humans, always involves multitasking. Any speaker must monitor social cues to be sure the listener is following; plan and produce content; worry about degrees of politeness and formality (i.e. social relationships in regard to distance and solidarity); forestall being interrupted; prepare for the listener's possible responses; and decide what aspects of meaning will be inferable from context and thus do not have to be explicitly stated in words. There are yet other things going on in conversation as well!

Undoubtedly we language users could, in some sense, be better communicators if we could do each of these things one at a time. But we can't. Language and communication demand multitasking.

Much work has always required multitasking. Think of being a waiter or waitress in a restaurant (or play the game *Diner Dash*). We are sure waiters and waitresses would like to think about one thing at a time. But that is what is called an unemployed waiter or waitress.

Video games like *World of WarCraft* also require multitasking. In the game, characters who play priests often heal and otherwise "buff" (put helpful spells on) the other players on their team. When you are in a dungeon with dozens of other people, it would be great to pay attention only to healing, your main skill. But in that case you, and your teammates who count on you, will be dead ("wiped" as they say). The priest must pay attention to the health of every other player, each of whom is a different type of character with different skills, so he or she can heal (or otherwise "buff") them in the right time and way. The priest also has to pay avid attention to the environment and how it is changing moment by moment as new enemies and challenges appear or the situation changes. And the priest has to engage in chat with the other players to make plans and adjust strategies with them, often on the fly.

Humans are made for multitasking. The claim that today's multitasking kids have a "new mind" is not true. They are using the old human mind. What is true is that today's world requires all of us, not just the young, to multitask in new ways and in some situations more than we ever have before. There are so many new technologies and so many more sources of information that people must be able to connect and integrate them in new ways.

Complexity

Our world today is more complex than ever. As we pointed out in previous chapters, we live amidst many interacting complex systems (systems made of many interacting variables with unpredictable outcomes), systems like global warming, the global economy, and global civilizational and religious conflicts. Experts and political leaders who cannot take into account many interacting variables at once are a danger. Who would vote for a President who could not multitask? Furthermore, we are talking about going well beyond multitasking to being able to collaborate with others to pool knowledge to deal with complex issues that resist simple solutions.

Real-time strategy (RTS) games

One type of video game is an excellent example of how multitasking is used to deal with complex systems. These are so-called "real-time strategy (RTS) games." RTS games (such as *StarCraft*, *Age of Empires*, *Rise of Nations*, and *Age of Mythology*) are among the most complex and demanding computer and video games made.

Let's take as our example the game *Rise of Nations* (*RoN*). In *RoN* players oversee a civilization of their choosing, a role that requires them to make a myriad of decisions (see Gee 2007c: ch. 6). They send their citizens out to gather resources (e.g. food, wood, minerals, gold) and use these resources to build domestic and military buildings and engage in various forms of research. In these buildings, they can train soldiers and other sorts of people (e.g. leaders, priests, scientists, and/or professors), as well as build military technologies and other sorts of apparatus.

As players gather and build, they can advance through different ages, allowing their civilization to achieve higher levels of complexity and sophistication. All the while they must go to war against or engage in diplomacy with other civilizations. All of this activity is done in real time. While the player builds up his or her civilization, other players (or the computer representing other players) are building up theirs as well. Players must decide when to attack or engage in diplomacy. Victory may come to the swift, that is, to those who attack early (a strategy called "rushing"), or to those who wait and patiently build up (a strategy called "turtling").

RoN allows the player to choose one of 18 civilizations (e.g. Aztecs, Bantu, British, Chinese, Egyptians, Maya, Nubians, Russians, Spanish, and others), each with different advantages and disadvantages. The player can play against one to seven opponents (other real people or computer-controlled civilizations). Players can move through eight ages from the Ancient Age to the Information Age, with various intervening ages such as the Medieval Age, the Gunpowder Age, and the Enlightenment Age.

Like all RTS games, *RoN* involves players in learning well over a hundred different commands, each connected to decisions that need to be made as they move through a myriad of different menus (there are 102 commands on the abridged list printed on a small sheet enclosed with the game). Players must operate at top speed if they are to keep up with skilled opponents who are building up civilizations simultaneously. *RoN* involves a great deal of micromanagement and decision making under time pressure.

RTS games like *RoN* require the player to anticipate and manage changes in many interacting variables from the perspective of several different civilizations. Players have to make some decisions that no real world leader has ever (yet) had to make. For example, a player has to decide whether to invest his or her civilization's resources in building technology or invest in other aspects of civilization first.

The world is becoming, with all its high-risk complex systems, like an RTS game. People in such a world need to think and act like RTS players. Our popular culture and its games are, in this case, more in tune with twenty-first century skills than are many of our leaders, researchers, and schools. It is an irony that in a world that requires big picture thinking and planning for both the short term and the long term, skills used in RTS games, we are trapped in countries (like the United States) with leaders who think only in the short term, namely, about the current quarter in which a company's stock has gone up or down, or the terms of office of politicians who often have to run for re-election before the true effects of their policies will ever be known.

So, multitasking is not the problem. All humans who could not multitask when they had to communicate, work, or hunt are gone, for good Darwinian reasons. We are multitaskers by nature, a good thing because the world requires it more and more.

The real issue, we believe, is this: how to manage our "attentional economy" in a world that makes more and more demands on our attention. The question is not multitasking, but when, where, and how to do it and do it well. How should we allocate our attentional resources, which are limited, in the face of more and more sources of information, forms of media, and pressing needs and problems in the world? When should we take breaks from quick bursts of alternating attention (as one must do in *RoN*) and engage in longer, drawn out periods of attention paid to fewer things (as one must do in *RoN* as well at the end of a play session when players pore over graphs and diagrams that capture and represent their actions in the game so they can form better strategies for their next play session)?

The attentional economy: More on polarization

Jack Fuller (2010), a Pulitzer Prize winning journalist has this to say about the future of news:

> Here is the deepest and, to many serious journalists, most disturbing truth about the future of news: The audience will control it. They will get the kind of news they choose. Not the kind they say they want, but the kind they actually choose (Fuller 2010: 5)

We all know printed newspapers are dying. People get their news more and more on the Internet. Furthermore, today, people can create their own news. They can create web sites that offer their own slant on the news or they can gather their own information on recent events. The pervasive use of cell phones with cameras means that everyday people can take the first pictures of significant events and offer the first accounts. There are web sites where people can pool their real-time observations about events (serious or trivial) as they unfold, as they can also do with Twitter and other social media (Shirky 2010).

What is happening to newspapers is part of a larger trend. In the literate social formation, people tended to consume more than they produced. Reading was always much more pervasive than writing. What information got shared with others, when that information was consequential and sensitive, was controlled by governments and other institutions.

In today's digital social formation, many people want to consume, produce, and share everything from news and entertainment; they want to design things and engage in citizen science with others on their own terms (Jenkins 2006a, 2006b; Shirky 2008, 2010). As we discussed in the previous chapter, modern businesses customize their products and services in terms of lifestyle niches and offer customers opportunities to produce and share with the company and other customers. But many digitally savvy people today do not want or need their consumption, production, and sharing controlled by businesses or institutions. They want to make and sell or freely give away their own products and ideas.

For example, in a game like *The Sims* players can design and sell or give away their own designs for landscapes, furniture, clothes, and other things (Gee & Hayes 2010). When they do, they add content to a game owned by a for-profit company (Maxis), a company who gets their services for free. Maxis provides some of the tools that players use to create and share content, and gives them mostly free rein in terms of what they can produce. While this is highly advantageous for the company, it is the sort of relationship more and more people want with businesses and governments.

There is a yet more important source today of the desire for consumption coupled with production and sharing. In modern economies, relatively few people can gain status "on market" (Gee *et al.* 1996; Toffler & Toffler 2006). Highly skilled people who innovate new knowledge, products, services, and markets (or who, at a professional level, help others to do so) can gain a good deal of wealth and power in a modern society in the global world. To the extent that status and a sense of worth are tied to wealth, such people get their status and sense of self-worth on market.

Many people cannot get status and a sense of agency, control, and self-worth from paid employment (Reich 1992, 2007). Such people can join interest-driven groups or passionate affinity spaces (Chapter 7) on the Internet, produce and share everything from music videos to political commentaries, find mentors and mentor others, and even organize and lead online communities whose members may number in the thousands. People engage in such activity not always or even normally for money, but for a sense of making a contribution, belonging, status, and worth.

In an earlier book (Gee & Hayes 2010), we discuss a woman in her sixties who is a shut-in because of poor health but who designs content for *The Sims*. Her designs, which she gives away, have been downloaded 17 million times and the "guest book" on her own site has one million "thank you's." Today, anyone can find interest-driven groups and passionate affinity spaces devoted to almost any topic, problem, product, interest, or value one can imagine.

Chapter 9 on how people organize around cat health offers as good an example as any. In such spaces, profit is not the main motive or, most of the time, any motive at all for participation. People gain status for their contributions, not their credentials or wealth. These people do not need official institutions (e.g. vets or materials distributed by veterinary clinics or by universities) as much as they once did. When they do use expert information and vets they do so on different terms and with different expectations. They do not expect to be treated as "mere consumers" who know nothing and will merely accept whatever they are told.

So, news is not the only area where people can choose among many more options than ever before and produce their own. This proliferation of choice, participation, and production comes with perils as well as possibilities. The peril in the case of news is typical. As there are more choices, more sites of production, and more groups organized around their own values, passions, perspectives, and interests, there is the peril that everyone listens only to the news, and the slant on the news, that they already agree with. Increasingly, they can join others with similar values and beliefs and hear no counter perspectives. They can even easily manufacture and distribute "news" through digital media by hyping or harping on single issues or so slanting the news that it becomes propaganda.

More generally, it is easier today than ever before, at least since humans left hunting and gathering groups, for people to communicate, consume, produce, and share with only other like-minded people. If you do not like one group's passion-fueled perspective on news, science, religion, or avocado carving, or the norms for participation they set, then join another group or start your own. If you do not care about starving children in Africa, you can ensure you will never hear about them as you customize and select your news in myriad ways. If you think they deserve their fate, you can join a group—a racist one, say—that supports your views and ignore everyone else. This was always possible, of course, but today with so many sources of information we all have to tune out a great deal of it, and our own values are one possible and enticing filter.

There is another peril, as well. You can join interest-driven groups, passionate affinity spaces, and social networks of all sorts devoted to anything, however trivial or important, whether it contributes to any greater good or not. You can find all your needs for socialization and entertainment met there. You can, if you like, be nourished there alone with others like yourself and pay no attention to wider causes or any civic good. People can become like one issue politicians.

The upside of joining a group devoted to a shared passion is how wonderfully effective and productive these groups can be for learning, belonging, and producing. The downside is that, in a like-minded or like-valued group, people tend to move toward extreme expressions of their shared values. That is the only way for individuals to gain distinctiveness in such a group and is facilitated by the likelihood that one will not often confront alternative values.

It is not surprising that in the United States today our politics is severely polarized (Bishop 2008). Conservatives can join other conservatives and communicate only with them. The same goes for liberals. They can consume, produce, and share only among like-minded people. Political choices become lifestyle choices, definitions of who is the same as oneself and who is not.

In the 1950s and 1960s, television offered three choices for national news and none of them catered to any one interest group's ideology. Everyone had to listen to pretty much the same thing and hear news accounts whose slant they did not always like. Today, anyone can get customized news that panders to one's favored ideology (or produce news accounts themselves) and no one needs to listen to even an attempt at "objective" reporting (we know that there is no such thing as true objectivity, but there are gradations of bias; certainly there is news reporting much closer to objectivity than Fox News, for instance).

This brings us back to the issue of difference and commonality. In the digital social formation, how can people come together for civic good across their passions, lifestyles, values, and niches? The literacy social formation, with its fixed texts and standardizing institutions, gave rise to large enterprises that created some degree of commonality among diverse people. The price was sometimes dishonoring diversity and a lack of flexibility and customization.

In the digital formation, as fixed interpretations and institutions weaken, the problem is the opposite. The digital social formation gives us a plethora of customized, highly interactive, differentiated, passion-sharing groups. The price can be a lack of common civic purpose, shared values, and commitment to the nation or humanity as a whole.

Of course, we are now in the midst of a transition. The literacy social formation is still powerful. The digital social formation is emerging. Their values and practices conflict in certain ways. The strength of one is the weakness of the other. Perhaps, but just perhaps, this could become a virtue.

The Tower of Babel

The Tower of Babel story in the Bible is a story about diversity and common purpose. The story represents the initial dilemma of humanity. Different languages divided them. The Tower of Babel was meant to ensure that they could not engage in common cause against God. Indeed, large common causes are difficult to sustain if there are no shared language and values. The literacy formation, with its eventual growth of institutions, spoke to this issue. The result was standardized languages in most countries— every other variety then just counts as a "dialect"—and, across the world, the use of an international language. First this language was Latin, then French, and now English.

There is a cost to an international language. It means that speakers of other languages can be colonized by the speakers of that language, especially the universal language's native speakers. Today, English dominates the Internet, but that is fast changing. As people settle into their own digital niches, as translation tools get better and as speakers of other languages (like Mandarin) come to greatly outnumber English speakers, the Internet and social media will accommodate a wide array of languages, from those with a small number of speakers to those with many. Speakers of any language will be able to create their own passionate affinity spaces, virtual worlds, and social media for themselves and nourish themselves there. They will be both in and out of the global world at the same time.

When humans faced the original Tower of Babel problem, the diversity of tongues, they invented ways to solve it through standardized languages, an international language, and formal institutions that standardized, regulated, and enforced norms. What will the solution to the new Tower of Babel problem be, to our myriad digital lifestyle and value niches?

In a sense we are returning to what Lévi-Strauss (1992) saw as the ideal human world: many diverse groups each working out a different way of being human, close enough to other groups to occasionally steal and borrow, but far enough away so as not to fight or homogenize into one bland whole. Of course, in the early days of humanity it was geography that created distance, today it is a lack of attention paid to causes, concerns, and groups other than our own in a world that offers too much for our limited minds to accommodate.

We do not want to lose the potential of this new Lévi-Straussian world. In our view, mitigating homogeneity and finding new and unique ways to be human are all to the good. Interest-driven groups, passionate affinity spaces, and social networks that allow everyone not just to consume, but to produce, participate, and share are all to the good. The weakening of single-minded expertise and the hold of formal institutions is also to the good. That is the possibility of the digital social formation.

Polarization is the peril. It is the same peril we humans faced with different languages. Can we find a solution that, unlike the one in the literacy social formation, unites without colonizing, achieves common action without top-down control?

There are, of course, many examples of digital media being used to organize large-scale efforts to aid people and engage in civic and global action (Shirky 2008, 2010). Natural disasters, war, civil unrest and revolutions, diseases, and instances of political deceit often now elicit large-scale efforts to collect and share information and to act through diverse and interconnected global networks. It is harder than ever for dictators and politicians to hide or restrict information. These networked efforts do not require the support of formal institutions, though many such institutions can participate.

While it is certainly true that the Internet allows for large-scale global action, there is a new problem here. People are good at responding to causes when their emotions are engaged. That is why the responses to disasters like the hurricanes in New Orleans or Haiti were so large. However, today, the disasters and suffering to which we emotionally respond are the outcomes of complex interacting variables. Intervening in ways that seem good and make us feel good can sometimes seriously backfire.

We get energized over low-paying, abusive sweatshops hiring young girls in Asia and use a massive Internet campaign to close them (Kristof & WuDunn 2009). The girls go back to impoverished villages and many end up abused in brothels into which kidnappers or economic circumstances have forced them. We get energized over the brothels and close them. The girls go back to villages where they are abused, get no health care, and often die because boys are seen, especially in bad times, as adding more value for economic and cultural survival than do girls. There is a bigger system at play here in which global economics, global politics, the status of women, poverty, and culture all play a role.

This example is one of many. Today, to forestall disasters or end evil we need to think about and engage with complex systems, a nexus of interacting variables, and not just about the emotional images we have seen of suffering. Let's call this "nexus thinking and action." Nexus thinking and action are not emotional and engaging in the way visions of human suffering are. They seem cold, technical, and rational.

As we said in the last chapter, Konrad Lorenz (2002, originally published in 1963) once argued that we humans would need to learn to feel empathy for people we cannot see face-to-face. Equally in our digital world, humans need to learn to feel emotional about and engaged with nexus thinking and action. This is not going to be easy. A nexus of complicated interacting variables just isn't "sexy" to most people. But if we do not learn this, even our best intentions will often lead to more disaster and suffering. The Internet can lead both to greater and more powerful emotional responses and to greater and deeper nexus thinking and action. But so far we are experiencing more of the former than the latter.

The digital world offers hope indeed. A world in which digital networks fire up for civic action and national and international causes and emergencies, but where different passionate affinity spaces work out distinctive ways to be human, with occasional borrowing and stealing from each other, sounds promising indeed.

In the emerging digital social formation can we find common purpose without forms of institutional standardization that mitigate difference and diversity? Can we find a new common and universal language that is based on shared meanings delivered in many different tongues, but translated by many different sources, human and digital, into usable resources for everyone through a variety of (albeit loosely connected) networks and groups? Perhaps, the Tower of Babel will then be turned into a resource not to save God from attack, but to save humanity from itself.

REFERENCES

Academy of Achievement (2010). *Clyde Tombaugh biography*. Available: www.achievement.org/autodoc/page/tom0bio-1 (accessed October 13, 2010).

Adams, M. J. (1990). *Beginning to read: Thinking and learning about print*. Cambridge, MA: MIT Press.

Allen, D. E. (1994). *The naturalist in Britain: A social history*. Princeton, NJ: Princeton University Press.

American Federation of Teachers (2003). The fourth-grade plunge: The cause. The cure. *American Educator* (Themed issue) 27(1). Available: www.aft.org/news-pubs/periodicals/ae/spring2003/index.cfm (accessed October 13, 2010).

Anderson, B. (2006). *Imagined communities*. London, New York: Verso.

Anderson, C. (2006). *The long tail: Why the future of business is selling less of more*. New York: Hyperion.

Anderson, J. M. (1971). *The grammar of case: Towards a localistic theory*. Cambridge: Cambridge University Press.

Andrews, E. L. (2008). Greenspan concedes error on regulation. *The New York Times*, October 23. Available: www.nytimes.com/2008/10/24/business/economy/24panel.html?_r=1 (accessed October 13, 2010).

Au, W. J. (2008). *The making of Second Life: Notes from the new world*. New York: HarperCollins.

Bakhtin, M. M. (1981). *The dialogic imagination*. Austin, TX: University of Texas Press.

Bakhtin, M. M. (1986). *Speech genres and other late essays*. Austin: University of Texas Press.

Barsalou, L. W. (1999). Language comprehension: Archival memory or preparation for situated action. *Discourse Processes*, 28: 61–80.

Bauerline, M. (2008). *The dumbest generation: How the digital age stupefies young Americans and jeopardizes our future (or don't trust anyone under 30)*. New York: Penguin.

Bauman, Z. (1998). *Globalization: The human consequences*. Cambridge: Polity Press.

Bauman, Z. (2000). *Individualized society*. Cambridge: Polity Press.

Bazerman, C. (1988). *Shaping written knowledge*. Madison: University of Wisconsin Press.

Beck, I. L., McKeown, M. G., & Kucan, L. (2002). *Bringing words to Life: Robust vocabulary instruction*. New York: Guilford Press.

Biemiller, A. (2003). Oral comprehension sets the ceiling on reading comprehension. *American Educator*, 27(1): 23, 44.

Binkenstein & Malan (2008). Basic theorycrafting. Available: http://elitistjerks.com/f47/t20314-basic_theorycrafting/#ixzz0o13FOJlL (accessed October 13, 2010).

Bishop, B. (2008). *The big sort: Why the clustering of like-minded America is tearing us apart*. New York: Houghton Mifflin.

Black, R. W. (2008). *Adolescents and online fan fiction*. New York: Peter Lang.

Boethius (2009). Forum rules. Message posted January 28 to http://elitistjerks.com/misc.php?do=cfrules (accessed October 15, 2010).

Botha, R. & Knight, C. (2009). *The prehistory of language*. Oxford: Oxford University Press.

Bowler, P. J. (1990). *Charles Darwin: The man and his influence*. Cambridge: Cambridge University Press.

Bransford, J. D. & Schwartz, D. L. (1999). Rethinking transfer: A simple proposal with multiple implications. In A. Iran-Nejad & P. D. Pearson (eds), *Review of research in education*, vol. 24 (pp. 61–100). Washington, DC: American Educational Research Association.

Brockman, J. (2010). A big question: "How is the Internet changing the way you think?" *Neiman Reports*, 64(2): 15–17.

Brown, P. (1988). *The body and society: Men, women, and sexual renunciation in early Christianity*. New York: Columbia University Press.

Brown, P. & Levinson, S. C. (1987). *Politeness: Some universals in language usage*. Cambridge: Cambridge University Press.

Burger, R. (1980). *Plato's Phaedrus: A defense of a philosophical art of writing*. Tuscaloosa, Alabama: University of Alabama Press.

Burke, K. (1993). *Rhetoric and ideology*. New York: Routledge.

Byrne, R. W. & Whiten, A. (1988). *Machiavellian intelligence: Social expertise and the evolution of intellect in monkeys, apes, and humans*. Oxford: Oxford University Press.

Cahill, T. (1996). *How the Irish saved civilization*. New York: Anchor.

Carr, N. (2010). *The shallows: What the Internet is doing to our brains*. New York: Norton.

Chall, J. S., & Jacobs, V. A. (2003). Poor children's fourth-grade slump. *American Educator*, 27(1). Available: www.aft.org/newspubs/periodicals/ae/spring2003/hirschsbclassic.cfm (accessed October 13, 2010).

Chall, J. S. Jacobs, V. A., & Baldwin, L. E. (1990). *The reading crisis: Why poor children fall behind*. Cambridge, MA: Harvard University Press.

Chaplin, E. (2006). The convention of captioning: W. G. Sebald and the release of the captive image. *Visual Studies*, 21(1): 42–53.

Chi, M., Feltovich, P., & Glaser, R. (1981). Categorization and representation of physics problems by experts and novices. *Cognitive Science*, 5(2): 121–152.

Chomsky, N. (1957). *Syntactic structures.* The Hague: Mouton.

Chomsky, N. (1986). *Knowledge of language: Its nature, origin, and use.* New York: Praeger.

Clark, A. (1989). *Microcognition: Philosophy, cognitive science, and parallel distributed processing.* Cambridge, MA: MIT Press.

Clark, H. H. (1996). *Using language.* Cambridge: Cambridge University Press.

Coles, G. (2000). *Misreading reading: The bad science that hurts children.* Portsmouth, NH: Heinemann.

Collins, C. (2005). Not ready for a Super Bowl spot: Rise of amateur ads. *The Christian Science Monitor*, February 7. Available: www.csmonitor.com/2005/0207/p01s02-ussc.html (accessed October 13, 2010).

Collins, H. & Evans, R. (2007). *Rethinking expertise.* Chicago, IL: University of Chicago Press.

Comrie, B. (1981). *Language universals and linguistic typology.* Chicago: University of Chicago Press.

Constant, D., Sproull, L. & Kiesler, S. (1996). The kindness of strangers: The usefulness of electronic weak ties for technical advice. *Organization Science*, 7: 119–135.

Consumers International (2008). *Toyota – Greenscrubbing Award for environmental impact.* Available: http://www.consumersinternational.org/our-work/social-responsibility/key-projects/holding-corporations-to-account/bad-company-awards/2008 (accessed October 15, 2010).

Crowley, K. & Jacobs, M. (2002). Islands of expertise and the development of family scientific literacy. In G. Leinhardt, K. Crowley, & K. Knutson (eds), *Learning conversations in museums* (pp. 333–356). Mahwah, NJ: Lawrence Erlbaum.

Dickinson, D. K., Golinkoff, R. M., & Hirsh-Pasek, K. (2010). Speaking out for language: Why language is central to reading development. *Educational Researcher*, 39(4): 305–310.

Dickinson, D. K. & Neuman, S. B. (eds) (2006). *Handbook of early literacy research*, vol. 2. New York: Guilford Press.

diSessa, A. A. (2000). *Changing minds: Computers, learning, and literacy.* Cambridge, MA: MIT Press.

Douglas, M. (1986). *How institutions think.* Syracuse NY: Syracuse University Press.

Drucker, P. F. (1993). *Post-capitalist society.* New York: Harder.

Duranti, A. (1997). *Linguistic anthropology.* Cambridge: Cambridge University Press.

Easley, D. & Kleinberg, J. (2010). *Networks, crowds, and markets: Reasoning about a highly connected world.* New York: Cambridge University Press.

Eisenberg, L. (2005). "Which image for Lorenz?" *American Journal of Psychiatry*, 162(9): 1760.

Entertainment Software Association (2010). *Essential facts about the computer and video game industry.* Washington: Author. Available: www.theesa.com/facts/game-player.asp (accessed October 13, 2010).

Federation of American Scientists (2006). *Harnessing the power of video games for learning.* Washington: Author.

Forsgren, S. (2008). *Addon Spotlight: DrDamage.* Available:: www.wow.com/2008/05/02/addon-spotlight-drdamage/#continued (accessed October 13, 2010).

Frank, T. (2000). *One market under God: Extreme capitalism, market populism, and the end of economic democracy.* New York: Doubleday.

Friedman, T. (2005). *The world is flat: A brief history of the twenty-first century.* New York: Farrar, Straus and Giroux.

Fuller, J. (2010). Feeling the heat: The brain holds clues for journalism. *Neiman Reports,* 64(2): 5–7.

Galison P. & Hevly B. (eds) (1992). *Big science: The growth of large-scale research.* Stanford, CA: Stanford University Press.

Gee, J. P. (1992). *The social mind: Language, ideology, and social practice.* New York: Bergin & Garvey.

Gee, J. P. (2000). Teenagers in new times: A new literacy studies perspective. *Journal of Adolescent & Adult Literacy,* 43(5): 412–420.

Gee, J. P. (2004). *Situated language and learning: A critique of traditional schooling.* London: Routledge.

Gee, J. P. (2006). Self-fashioning and shape-shifting: Language, identity, and social class. In D. Alverman, K. Hinchman, D. Moore, S. Phelps, & D. Waff (eds), *Reconceptualizing the literacies in adolescents' lives,* 2nd edn (pp. 165–186). Hillsdale, NJ: Erlbaum.

Gee, J. P. (2007a). *Social linguistics and literacies: Ideology in discourses,* 3rd edn. London: Taylor & Francis.

Gee, J. P. (2007b). *What video games have to teach us about learning and literacy,* 2nd edn. New York: Palgrave/Macmillan.

Gee, J. P. (2007c). *Good video games and good learning: Collected essays on video games, learning, and literacy.* New York: Peter Lang.

Gee, J. P. (2008a). Decontextualized language and the problem of school failure. In C. Compton-Lilly (ed.), *Breaking the silence: Recognizing the social and cultural resources students bring to the classroom* (pp. 24–33). Newark, DE: International Reading Association.

Gee, J. P. (2008b). *Getting over the slump: Innovation strategies to promote children's learning.* New York: The Joan Ganz Cooney Center.

Gee, J. P. (2010). *An introduction to discourse analysis: Theory and method,* 3rd edn. London: Routledge.

Gee, J. P. & Crawford, V. (1998). Two kinds of teenagers: Language, identity, and social class. In D. Alvermann, K. Hinchman, D. Moore, S. Phelps, & D. Waff (eds), *Reconceptualizing the literacies in adolescents' lives* (pp. 225–245). Hillsdale, NJ: Erlbaum.

Gee, J. P. & Goodhart, W. (1988). American Sign Language and the human biological capacity for language. In M. Strong (ed.), *Language learning and deafness* (pp. 49–74). Cambridge: Cambridge University Press.

Gee, J. P. & Hayes, E. R. (2010). *Women and gaming: The Sims and 21st century learning.* New York: Palgrave/Macmillan.

Gee, J. P., Hull, G., & Lankshear, C. (1996). *The new work order: Behind the language of the new capitalism*. Boulder, CO: Westview.

Gee, J. P., Allen, A.-R., & Clinton, K. (2001). Language, class, and identity: Teenagers fashioning themselves through language. *Linguistics and Education*, 12(2): 175–194.

Gladwell, M. (2008). *Outliers: The story of success*. New York: Little, Brown.

Goody, J. (1986). *The logic of writing and the organization of society*. Cambridge: Cambridge University Press.

Goody, J. (1988). *The interface between the written and the oral*. Cambridge: Cambridge University Press.

Goody, J. & Watt, I. P. (1963). The consequences of literacy. *Comparative Studies in History and Society*, 5: 304–345.

Gore, A. (2006). *An inconvenient truth: The planetary emergency of global warming and what we can do about it*. New York: Rodale Books.

Gould, S. J. (1985). *The flamingo's smile: Reflections in natural history*. New York: W. W. Norton & Company.

Graff, H. J. (1979). *The literacy myth: Literacy and social structure in the 19th century city*. New York: Academic Press.

Graff, H. J. (1987). *The labyrinths of literacy: Reflections on literacy past and present*. New York: The Falmer Press.

Graff, H. J., Mackinnon, A., Sandin, B., & Winchester, I. (eds) (2009). *Understanding literacy in its historical contexts: Socio-cultural history and the legacy of Egil Johansson*. Lund, Sweden: Nordic Academic Press.

Grann, D. (2010). *The devil and Sherlock Holmes: Tales of murder, madness, and obsession*. New York: Doubleday.

Granovetter, M. S. (1973). The strength of weak ties. *American Journal of Sociology*, 78(6): 1360–1380.

Greenberg, J. H. (1978). *Universals of human language*, vol. 1: *Method and theory*, vol. 2: *Phonology*, vol. 3: *Word structure*, vol. 4: *Syntax*. Stanford, CA: Stanford University Press.

Greider, W. (1997). *One world, ready or not: The manic logic of global capitalism*. New York: Simon & Schuster.

Grosjean, F. & Lane, H. (eds) (1980). *Recent perspectives in American Sign Language*. Hillsdale, NJ: Erlbaum.

Gumperz, J. J. (ed.) (1982a). *Language and social identity*. Cambridge: Cambridge University Press.

Gumperz, J. J. (1982b). *Discourse strategies*. Cambridge: Cambridge University Press.

Guthrie, W. K. C. (1986). *A history of Greek philosophy, vol. 4: Plato: The man and his dialogues: Earlier period*. Cambridge: Cambridge University Press.

Habermas, J. (1984). *Theory of communicative action*, vol. 1 (T. McCarthy, trans.). London: Heinemann.

Hacking, I. (1990). *The taming of chance*. Cambridge: Cambridge University Press.

Halliday, M. A. K. & Hasan, R. (1989). *Language, context, and text: Aspects of language as a social-semiotic perspective*. Oxford: Oxford University Press.

Hare, R. M. (1982). *Plato*. New York: Oxford University Press.

Hargittai, E. (2010). Digital na(t)ives? Variation in Internet skills and uses among members of the "Net Generation." *Sociological Inquiry*, 80(1): 92–113.

Hart, T. & Risely, B. (1995). *Meaningful differences in the early experience of young American children.* Baltimore: Brookes.

Havelock, E. (1976). *Preface to Plato.* Cambridge, MA: Harvard University Press.

Havelock, E. A. (1986). *The muse learns to write: Reflections on orality and literacy from antiquity to the present.* New Haven: Yale University Press.

Hayes, E. & Gee, J. P. (2010). Public pedagogy through video games: Design, resources, and affinity spaces. In J. A. Sandlin, B. D. Schultz, & J. Burdick (eds), *Handbook of public pedagogy* (pp. 185–193). New York: Routledge.

Haythornthwaite, C. (2002). Building social networks via computer networks: Creating and sustaining distributed learning communities. In K. A. Renninger & W. Shumar (eds), *Building virtual communities: Learning and change in cyberspace* (pp. 159–190). Cambridge: Cambridge University Press.

Heath, S. B. (1983). *Ways with words: Language, life, and work in communities and class-rooms.* Cambridge: Cambridge University Press.

Hill, C. & Larsen, E. (2000). *Children and reading tests.* Stamford, CT: Ablex.

Howe, J. (2008a). *Crowdsourcing: Why the power of the crowd is driving the future of business.* New York: Crown Business.

Howe, J. (2008b). Can we crowdsource medical expertise? August 26 [Blog post] Available http://crowdsourcing.typepad.com/cs/2008/08/can-we-crowds-1.html (accessed October 13, 2010).

Hull, G. & Nelson, M. (2005). Locating the semiotic power of multimodality. *Written Communication*, 22(2): 1–38.

Ion Storm (2000). *Deus Ex Manual.* London: Eidos Interactive. Available: http://gamecontentgreen.yummy.net/deusexdemo/doc/Deusexmanual.pdf (accessed October 13, 2010).

Isaacs, J. (2006). *Australian dreaming: 40,000 years of Aboriginal history.* Chatswood, NSW, Australia: New Holland Publishing.

Ito, M., Baumer, S., Bittanti, M., boyd, d., Cody, R., Herr-Stephenson, B., Horst, H. A., Lange, P. G., Mahendran, D., Martinez, K. Z., Pascoe, C. J., Perkel, D., Robinson, L., Sims, C., & Tripp, L. (2010). *Hanging out, messing around, and geeking out: Kids living and learning with new media.* Cambridge, MA: MIT Press.

Jenkins, H. (2006a). *Confronting the challenges of participatory culture: Media education for the 21st century.* Chicago: MacArthur Foundation.

Jenkins, H. (2006b). *Convergence culture: Where old and new media collide.* New York: New York University Press.

Jewitt, C. (2006). *Technology, literacy and learning: A multimodal approach.* London and New York: Routledge.

Jewitt, C. & Kress, G. (eds) (2003). *Multimodal literacy.* New York: Peter Lang.

Johansson, E. (1977). *The history of literacy in Sweden.* Umeå: Umeå University Press.

Johnson, S. (2006). *Everything bad is good for you: How today's popular culture is actually making us smarter.* New York: Riverhead.

Johnson, S. & Kwak, J. (2010). *13 Bankers: The Wall Street takeover and the next financial meltdown*. New York: Pantheon Books.

Juel, C. (1988). Learning to read and write: A longitudinal study of 54 children from first to fourth grades. *Journal of Educational Psychology*, 80: 437–447.

Juel, C., Griffith, P., & Gough, P. B. (1986). Acquisition of literacy: A longitudinal study of children in first and second grade. *Journal of Educational Psychology* 78: 243–255.

Juul, J. (2009). *A casual revolution: Reinventing video games and their players*. Cambridge, MA: The MIT Press.

Kanigel, R. (1997). *The one best way: Frederick Winslow Taylor and the enigma of efficiency*. New York: Penguin.

Kelly, K. (1994). *Out of control: The new biology of machines, social systems, and the economic world*. Reading, MA: Addison-Wesley.

Kermode, F. (1979). *The genesis of secrecy: On the interpretation of narrative*. Cambridge, MA: Harvard University Press.

Kintsch, W. (1998). *Comprehension: A paradigm for cognition*. New York: Cambridge University Press.

Knapp, S. (2003). *Plant discoveries: A botanist's voyage through plant exploration*. Somerville, MA: Firefly Press.

Kress, G. (2000). Multimodality. In B. Cope & M. Kalantzis (eds), *Multiliteracies: Literacy learning and the design of social futures* (pp. 182–202). Melbourne: Macmillan.

Kress, G. (2003). *Literacy in the new media age*. London: Routledge.

Kress, G. & van Leeuwen, T. (1996). *Reading images: The grammar of visual design*. London: Routledge.

Kristof, N. D. & WuDunn, S. (2009). *Half the sky: Turning oppression into opportunity for women worldwide*. New York: Knopf.

Labov, W. (1972). *Sociolinguistic patterns*. Philadelphia: University of Pennsylvania Press.

Lakoff, G. (1987). *Women, fire, and dangerous things: What categories reveal about the mind*. Chicago: University of Chicago Press.

Lakoff, G. & Johnson, M. (1980). *Metaphors we live by*. Chicago: University of Chicago Press.

Lam, W. S. E. (2009). Multiliteracies on instant messaging in negotiating local, translocal, and transnational affiliations: A case of an adolescent immigrant. *Reading Research Quarterly*, 44(4): 377–397.

Laqueur, T. (1990). *Making sex: Body and gender from the Greeks to Freud*. Cambridge, MA: Harvard University Press.

Lareau, A. (2003). *Unequal childhoods: Class, race, and family life*. Berkeley, CA: University of California Press.

Latour, B. (1987). *Science in action*. Cambridge, MA: Harvard University Press.

Latour, B. (1999). *Pandora's hope: Essays on the reality of science studies*. Cambridge, MA: Harvard University Press.

Leach, W. (1993). *Land of desire: Merchants, power, and the rise of a new American culture*. New York: Vintage.

Leadbeater, C. & Miller, P. (2004). *The Pro-Am revolution: How enthusiasts are changing our society and economy*. London: Demos.

Lemke, J. (1998). Multiplying meaning: Visual and verbal semiotics in scientific text. In J. R. Martin & R. Veel (eds), *Reading science: Critical and functional perspectives on discourses of science* (pp. 87–113). London: Routledge.

Lenhardt, A. & Madden, M. (2005). *Teen content creators and consumers*. Washington, DC: Pew Internet & American Life Project. Available: www.pewInternet.org/PPF/r/166/report_display.asp (accessed October 13, 2010).

Levinson, S. C. (1983). *Pragmatics*. Cambridge: Cambridge University Press.

Lévi-Strauss, C. (1975). *Tristes tropiques*. New York: Athenaeum.

Lévi-Strauss, C. (1992). *The view from afar* (J. Neugroschel, trans.). Chicago, IL: University of Chicago Press.

Lewis, M. (2010). *The big short: Inside the Doomsday machine*. New York: W. W. Norton & Co.

Lin, N. (2001). *Social capital: A theory of social structure and action*. New York: Cambridge University Press.

Lockwood, M. (2007). *The Sims* phenomenon, January 24. Available: http://ezinearticles.com/?The-Sims-Phenomenon&id=430065 (accessed October 13, 2010).

Lorenz, K. (2002). *On aggression*. London: Routledge.

Lovejoy, A. (1933). *The great chain of being: A study of the history of an idea*. Cambridge, MA: Harvard University Press.

Lucier, P. (2009). The professional and the scientist in nineteenth-century America. *Isis*, 100(4): 699–732.

Lyons, J. (1977). *Semantics*. Cambridge: Cambridge University Press.

Martin, J. R. (1990). Literacy in science: Learning to handle text as technology. In F. Christe (ed.), *Literacy for a changing world* (pp. 79–117). Melbourne: Australian Council for Educational Research.

McGrail, M. R., Rickard, C. M., & Jones, R. (2006). Publish or perish: A systematic review of interventions to increase academic publication rates. *Higher Education Research and Development*, 25(1): 19–35.

Milroy, J. & Milroy, L. (1985). *Authority in language: Investigating language prescription and standardisation*. London: Routledge.

Mims, F. M. III (1999). Amateur science—Strong tradition, bright future. *Science*, 284 (5411). Available: www.sciencemag.org/cgi/content/full/284/5411/55 (accessed October 13, 2010).

Moss, P. A., Pullin, D. C., Gee, J. P., Haertel, E. H., & Young, L. J. (eds) (2008). *Assessment, equity, and opportunity to learn*. Cambridge: Cambridge University Press.

Myers, G. (1990). *Writing biology: Texts in the social construction of scientific knowledge*. Madison, WI: University of Wisconsin Press.

Nass, C. (2010). Thinking about multitasking: It's what journalists need to do. *Neiman Reports*, 64(2): 11–12.

National Reading Panel (2000). *Teaching children to read: An evidence-based assessment of the scientific research literature on reading and its implications for reading instruction*.

Reports of the subgroups. Rockville, MD: National Institute of Child Health and Human Development.

Neuman, S. B. (2010). Lessons from my mother: Reflections on the National Early Literacy panel report. *Educational Researcher*, 39(4): 301–304.

Neuman, S. B. & Celano, D. (2006). The knowledge gap: Implications of leveling the playing field for low-income and middle-income children. *Reading Research Quarterly*, 41(2): 176–201.

Olson, D. R. (1996). *The world on paper: The conceptual and cognitive implications of writing and reading.* Cambridge: Cambridge University Press.

Olson, G. M., Zimmerman, A., & Bos, N. (2008). *Scientific collaboration on the Internet.* Cambridge, MA: MIT Press.

Ong, W. J. (1982). *Orality and literacy: The technologizing of the word.* London: Methuen.

Owen, D. (1985). *None of the above: Behind the myth of scholastic aptitude.* Boston: Houghton Mifflin.

Parker, G. (2002). *Cross-functional teams: Working with allies, enemies, and other strangers.* San Francisco: Jossey-Bass.

Parry, M. (1971). *The making of Homeric verse: The collected papers of Milman Parry.* Oxford: Clarendon Press.

Pattison, R. (1982). *On literacy: The politics of the word from Homer to the age of rock.* Oxford: Oxford University Press.

Pickering, A. (1995). *The mangle of practice: Time, agency, and science.* Chicago: University of Chicago Press.

Pinker, S. (1994). *The language instinct: How the mind creates language.* New York: William Morrow.

Plowdell, J. (2006) Marketing ploy turns on owner. *Marketing Shift*, April 4 (Blog post). Available: www.marketingshift.com/2006/4/marketing-ploy-turns-on-owner.cfm (accessed October 13, 2010).

Price, D. J. D. (1963). *Little science, big science.* New York: Columbia University Press.

Pullum, G. K. (1991). *The great Eskimo vocabulary hoax and other irreverent essays on the study of language.* Chicago, IL: University of Chicago Press.

Ransom, J. C. (1941). *The New Criticism.* Norfolk, CT: New Directions.

Reich, R. B. (1992). *The work of nations.* New York: Vintage Books.

Reich, R. B. (2007). *Supercapitalism: The transformation of business, democracy, and everyday life.* New York: Vintage Books.

Rifkin, J. (2000). *The age of access: The new culture of hypercapitalism where all of life is a paid-for experience.* New York: Jeremy P. Tarcher/Putnam.

Rose, J. (2001). *The intellectual life of the British working classes.* New Haven, CT: Yale University Press.

Rowe, C. J. (1986). *Plato: Phaedrus*, translation and commentary. Warminster, UK: Aris and Philips.

Saenger, P. (1997). *Space between words: The origins of silent reading.* Stanford, CA: Stanford University Press.

Sampson, G. (1990). *Writing systems: a linguistic introduction*, Stanford, CA: Stanford University Press.

Saussure, F. de (1916). *Cours de linguistique générale*. Paris: Payot. (English translation published as *A course in general linguistics* [Wade Baskin, trans.]. New York: McGraw-Hill, 1959.)

Schleppegrell, M. (2004). *The language of schooling: A functional linguistics perspective*. Mahwah, NJ: Lawrence Erlbaum.

Scollon, R. & Scollon, S. W. (1981). *Narrative, literacy, and face in interethnic communication*. Norwood, NJ: Ablex.

Scribner, S. & Cole, M. (1981). *The psychology of literacy*. Cambridge, MA: Harvard University Press.

Seabrook, J. (2000). *Nobrow: The culture of marketing, the marketing of culture*. New York: Vintage Books.

Sénéchal, M., Ouellette, G., & Rodney, D. (2006). The misunderstood giant: On the predictive role of early vocabulary to future reading. In D. K. Dickinson & S. B. Neuman (eds), *Handbook of early literacy research*, vol. 2 (pp. 173–182). New York: Guilford Press.

Sennett, R. (1977). *The fall of public man*. New York: Knopf.

Shaffer, D. W. (2007). *How computer games help children learn*. New York: Palgrave/Macmillan.

Shapin, S. & Schaffer, S. (1985). *Leviathan and the air-pump*. Princeton: Princeton University Press.

Shirky, C. (2008). *Here comes everybody: The power of organizing without organizations*. New York: Penguin.

Shirky, C. (2010). *Cognitive surplus: Creativity and generosity in a connected age*. New York: Penguin.

Shrum, W., Genuth, J., & Chompalov, I. (2007). *Structures of scientific collaboration*. Cambridge, MA: MIT Press.

Sinclair, R. K. (1988). *Democracy and participation in Athens*. Cambridge: Cambridge University Press.

Smith, D. L. (2007). *Why we lie: The evolutionary roots of deception and the unconscious mind*. New York: Macmillan.

Snow, C. E. (1991). The theoretical basis for relationships between language and literacy in development. *Journal of Research in Childhood Education,* 6(1): 5–10.

Squire, K. (2008). Video games and education: Designing learning systems for an interactive age. *Educational Technology,* 48(2): 17–26.

Star, S. L. (1989). *Regions of the mind: Brain research and the quest for scientific certainty*. Stanford, CA: Stanford University Press.

Starr, P. (1982). *The social transformation of American medicine: The rise of a sovereign profession and the making of a vast industry*. New York: Basic Books.

Steinberger, P. J. (2005). *The idea of the state*. Cambridge: Cambridge University Press.

Steinkuehler, C. A. & Duncan, S. C. (2008). Scientific habits of mind in virtual worlds. *Journal of Science Education and Technology,* 17(6): 530–543.

Steinkuehler, C. & Williams, D. (2006). Where everybody knows your (screen) name: Online games as "third places." *Journal of Computer-Mediated Communication,*

11(4). Available: http://jcmc.indiana.edu/vol11/issue4/steinkuehler.html (accessed October 13, 2010).

Stossel, J. (2008). Government stifles the wisdom of crowds. *The Freeman: Ideas on Liberty* 58(7). Available: www.thefreemanonline.org/columns/give-me-a-break-government-stifles-the-wisdom-of-crowds/# (accessed October 13, 2010).

Street, B. (1984). *Literacy in theory and practice.* Cambridge: Cambridge University Press.

Stross, N. (2010, July 9). Computers at home: Educational hope vs. teenage reality. *The New York Times,* July 9. Available: www.nytimes.com/2010/07/11/business/11digi.html?src=busln (accessed October 13, 2010).

Surowiecki, J. (2004). *The wisdom of crowds: Why the many are smarter than the few and how collective wisdom shapes business, economies, societies and nations.* Boston, MA: Little, Brown.

Tannen, D. (1985). Relative focus on involvement in oral and written discourse. In D. R. Olson, N. Torrance, & A. Hildyard (eds), *Literacy, language, and learning: The nature and consequences of reading and writing* (pp. 124–147). Cambridge: Cambridge University Press.

Taylor, A. E. (2001). *Plato: The man and his work.* Mineola, NY: Dover Publications.

Thurow, L. C. (1999). *Building wealth: The new rules for individuals, companies, and nations in a knowledge-based economy.* New York: HarperCollins.

TIMSS (2000a). *TIMSS 1999 International Science Report: Findings from IEA's Repeat of the Third International Mathematics and Science Study at the Eighth Grade.* Chestnut Hill, MA: Boston College.

TIMSS (2000b). *TIMSS 1999 International Mathematics Report: Findings from IEA's Repeat of the Third International Mathematics and Science Study at the Eighth Grade.* Chestnut Hill, MA: Boston College.

Toffler, A. & Toffler, H. (2006). *Revolutionary wealth: How it will be created and how it will change our lives.* New York: Knopf.

Tomasello, M. (1999). *The cultural origins of human cognition.* Cambridge, MA: Harvard University Press.

Wagner, C. S. (2008). *The new invisible college: Science for development.* Washington DC: Brookings Institution.

Wasik, B. (2009). *And then there's this: How stories live and die in viral culture.* New York: Viking.

Weidensaul, S. (2007). *Of a feather: A brief history of American birding.* Orlando, FL: Harcourt.

Wertsch, J. V. (1998). *Mind as action.* Oxford: Oxford University Press.

Westfall, R. (1993). *The life of Isaac Newton.* Cambridge: Cambridge University Press.

Whitley, B. (2009). Could texting slang be good for kids? *The Christian Science Monitor,* March 3. Available: www.csmonitor.com/Innovation/Horizons/2009/0303/could-texting-slang-be-good-for-kids (accessed October 13, 2010).

Williams, B. A. O. (1999). *Plato.* New York: Routledge.

Wimsatt, W. K. & Beardsley. M. C. (1946). The intentional fallacy. *Sewanee Review,* 54, 468–488.

Wolfson, N. (1989). *Perspectives: Sociolinguistics and TESOL.* Cambridge, MA: Newbury House.

Zane, R. (2005). Ziff Davis video game survey: Gamers continue to cut TV viewing [Press release], August 9. Available: www.ziffdavis.com/press/releases/050809.0.html (accessed October 13, 2010).

INDEX

abilities 9, 15–16
Aboriginals 50
abstract 10–11, 12
academic language 23, 54, 60, 63
alphabets 17–18
amateurs: authority 96; digital media 102–3; experts 76, 94–6; modern science 100; passionate affinity spaces 71–2; theory crafting 85
American Sign Language 14, 21–2, 115
anonymity 2–3, 32
Aristotle 51–2
art 40
assessment 68
astronomy 103
attention 137, 138–40
audience 3–4
audio recording 9
authority: Church 56; digital media 125; literate culture 123, 124; oral culture 122; religion 51; removed 53; science 51; trust 48–9; veterinarians 96; written language 2, 26–7
authors 29–30, 46, 98–9
avatars 37–8, 79, 130

Bazerman, C. 65
Bible 56
big science 102
bonding 23–5, 30–2, 34, 92, 97
books 55, 99
Burke, K. 40

canonical literature 38, 125, 133
capacity 8, 135
capitalism 107–8, 118
careers 109
cats 89, 90
children 9, 16, 105
Chomsky, Noam 7
Church 51–2
citizenship 110
civic spaces 89
Civilization 70
co-citizenship 127–9, 140
collaboration: academic language 63; amateurs 103; information 44; mods 87; new capitalism 108; schools 67; theory crafting 85; veterinarians 96; *World of Warcraft (WoW)* 81–2
collective experience 92–4, 95–6
communication: co-citizenship 128; control 139; corporate bodies 29–30; differences 127; essays 27–8; experiences 114; face-to-face 9, 121; language 6–7; literacy 16; multitasking 135; relationships 24–5; technology 133; Tower of Babel 141–2
competition 102–3
complex systems 44, 72–3, 82, 136, 142
comprehension: language 116, 117; skills 17; social languages 58–61; vocabulary 57; words 115
Consumers International 120
consumption 3, 56, 138